THE THIRD RECONSTRUCTION

THE THIRD RECONSTRUCTION

Moral Mondays,
Fusion Politics, and the Rise
of a New Justice Movement

—◦—

The Reverend Dr.
William J. Barber II

with Jonathan Wilson-Hartgrove

Beacon Press
Boston

Beacon Press
Boston, Massachusetts
www.beacon.org

Beacon Press books
are published under the auspices of
the Unitarian Universalist Association of Congregations.

19 18 17 16   8 7 6 5 4 3 2 1

This book is printed on acid-free paper that meets the uncoated paper
ANSI/NISO specifications for permanence as revised in 1992.

Text design by Wilsted & Taylor Publishing Services

Frontispiece photo by Phil Fonville

Library of Congress Cataloging-in-Publication Data

Barber, William J., II, author. | Wilson-Hartgrove, Jonathan, author.
The third reconstruction : Moral Mondays, fusion politics, and the
    rise of a new justice movement / the Reverend Dr. William J. Barber II
    with Jonathan Wilson-Hartgrove.
Includes bibliographical references and index.
ISBN 978-0-8070-8360-4 (hardback) | ISBN 978-0-8070-8362-8 (ebook)
1. Barber, William J., II. 2. African American civil rights workers—North
    Carolina—Biography. 3. Civil rights movements—United States.
    4. Civil rights—Religious aspects—Christianity. 5. Christianity
    and politics—United States.
BR516 .B337 2016   277.3/083—dc23

For the thousands who've sacrificed
to make a new "we" possible

And for Al McSurely and Ashley Osment,
who trusted the evidence of things not seen

CONTENTS

Go Home

LATE AUGUST in North Carolina is harvest time for tobacco growers. Long before the sun rises above the longleaf pines, the air is already thick and heavy in the fields of the eastern sandhills, where I was raised. Men and women roll up their sleeves and bend their backs to prime to-bacco, taking the bottom leaves first. I grew up in these fields, listening to the songs people hum when they know there's work to be done and the day is only going to get hotter. Some days I still wake up humming those songs.

August 28, 2013, I woke up at home in North Carolina. It had been a long, hot summer, and my body was tired. But as a mother of the church in Montgomery, Alabama, famously told Dr. Martin Luther King during the bus boycott, even though my feet were tired, my soul was rested. I woke up that morning humming a song I learned from mothers of the church in eastern North Carolina.

> I've got a feeling everything's gonna be all right.
> Oh I've got a feeling everything's gonna be all right.
> I've got a feeling everything's gonna be all right.
> Be all right, be all right, be all right.

Four days before, I'd been in Washington, DC, for the national commemoration of 1963's March on Washington. Fifty years after that historic day when millions of Americans heard Dr. King's dream on national television for the first time, civil rights leaders from around the country gathered to commemorate the achievements of freedom fighters who gave so much half a century ago to guarantee the opportunities we often take for granted today. I sat alongside a great hero of that era, Julian Bond, commenting on the day's celebrations for Melissa Harris-Perry on MSNBC.

But as soon as the festivities were over, I knew I had to go home.

I had been invited to go to Washington because Moral Mondays had gained national attention during that summer of 2013. On April 29, 2013, sixteen close colleagues and I had been arrested at the North Carolina statehouse for exercising our constitutional right to publicly instruct our legislators. We did not call it a Moral Monday when we went to the legislature building that day. In fact, it took us nearly three weeks to name what started with that simple act of protest. But when a small group of us stood together, refusing to accept an extreme makeover of state government that we knew would harm the most vulnerable among us, it was like a spark in a warehouse full of cured, dry tobacco leaves.

The following Monday, hundreds returned to the statehouse and twice as many people were arrested. Word of a mass movement spread among justice-loving people throughout North Carolina, igniting thousands who knew from their own experience that something was seriously wrong. Throughout the hot, wet summer of 2013, tens of thousands of people came for thirteen consecutive Moral Mondays. By the end of the legislative session, nearly a thousand people had been arrested in the largest wave of mass civil disobedience since the lunch counter sit-ins of 1960.

Those Moral Monday rallies were on my mind as I hummed the old spiritual that late August morning. Fifty years earlier, in Indianapolis, Indiana, my mother had gone into labor on this very day. The joke in my family is that I, the child in her womb, heard that people were marching for jobs and justice in Washington, so I decided to wait for them before my entrance into the world. By the time I was born two days later, my parents' friends and coworkers who had made the long trip to Washington were back home. They had heeded Dr. King's words:

> Go back . . . knowing that somehow this situation can and will be changed.

Going back home, they did the painstaking work of building communities committed to justice, educating neighbors about issues that affect the common good, and organizing poor people to register, vote, and speak out in their communities. As inspiring as Dr. King was, historians are clear that it was not him alone, but rather the thousands of unnamed people like my parents who turned the tide in America after the March on Washington, guaranteeing the passage of the Civil Rights Act in 1964 and, after Bloody Sunday in Selma the following spring, the Voting Rights Act of 1965. In fact, it was my father's commitment to go home and labor in forgotten fields that led him and my mother to return to North Carolina in the late 1960s, sending me to integrate the public schools in Washington County. I was drafted into the justice struggle before I ever had a chance to know anything else. I learned to be a freedom fighter by going home.

Half a century later, I found myself a leader in the reemerging Southern freedom movement, trying to understand a mass movement that had erupted in response to twenty-first-century injustice in my own home state. Moral Mondays had not "just happened." They resulted from the efforts of 140 organizations that had worked together as a grassroots coalition for seven years. When crowds chanted, "Thank you! We love you!" each week to the scores of arrestees leaving the legislature building in Department of Corrections buses, they were cheering on their pastors, their union leaders, their professors, and their grandmothers. We didn't just know one another. We were family.

But as much as I knew the people and understood the long, hard organizing work that had made Moral Mondays happen, I did not know how to explain this sudden explosion of resistance. Though it grew out of the familiar ground of freedom, something new was happening before our eyes. Like our foreparents who marched on Washington, we in North Carolina were caught up by the zeitgeist in something bigger than ourselves—something bigger, even, than our understanding. But we knew one thing without a doubt: we had found the essential struggle of our time. Inspired by nothing less than God's dream, we were ready to go home and do the long, hard work of building up a new justice movement to save the soul of America.

So I was at home on August 28, 2013—that Wednesday when we looked back to remember the fiftieth anniversary of the March on Washington. Our Forward Together Moral Movement held thirteen simultaneous rallies in each of North Carolina's congressional districts that day, bringing together tens of thousands of people who had been mobilized for action through Moral Mondays. We were black, white and brown, women and men, rich and poor, gay and straight, documented and undocumented, employed and unemployed, doctors and patients, people of faith and people who struggle with faith. We were, it seemed to me as I drove between rallies in Greensboro, Lincolnton, and Charlotte, a glimpse of Dr. King's dream—of the republic that, though promised and longed for, has never yet been. Baptized in the fires of mass demonstration, we were a fusion coalition of people committed to reconstructing America itself.

On national television, the networks broadcast commemorative speeches and historical reflections on Dr. King and the civil rights movement. Much of it was interesting history, I'm sure. But I witnessed something far more inspiring at home in North Carolina on the fiftieth anniversary of the March on Washington. I came home to the beginnings of a Third Reconstruction. After America's First Reconstruction was attacked by the lynch mobs of white supremacists in the 1870s, it took nearly a hundred years for a Second Reconstruction to emerge in the civil rights movement. Though we ended Jim Crow segregation in the 1960s, structural inequality became more sophisticated in the backlash against the movement's advances. We have a black man in the White House that was built by slaves, but the wealth divide that is rooted in our history of race-based slavery is more extreme than it ever has been. Nothing less than a Third Reconstruction holds the promise of healing our nation's wounds and birthing a better future for all. But we're not just waiting for it. We've seen what it looks like.

This book is about the Forward Together Moral Movement that began in North Carolina, gained attention through Moral Mondays, and has spread to statehouses and communities throughout America since the summer of 2013. As a first-person account of the events that led up to and beyond Moral Mondays, it is my memoir of the movement.

But this is not a story about me. The most important word in the justice vocabulary is always "we." This is the story of how some unlikely friends joined hands to reclaim the possibility of democracy in the face of corporate-financed extremism. It is an introduction to the fusion politics that give me hope for a future beyond the dead-end of partisan politics in America today.

Because we can never know the ecstasy of true hope without attending to the tragic realities of the poor and forgotten, this is also necessarily a book about what is wrong in America. Among other reasons, we must heed Dr. King's call to go home because policy analysis inside the Beltway has become detached from the lived experience of millions of Americans who live and die poor in the richest nation that the world has ever seen. I am not a politician. I am a pastor. The job of a pastor is to touch people where they are hurting and to do what is possible to bind up their wounds. You can only do this sort of work locally—among people whose names you know and who, likewise, know you. But you cannot do it honestly without at some point becoming a prophet. Something inside the human spirit cries out against the injustice of inequality when you know people who have to choose between food and medicine in a country where CEOs make more in an hour than their lowest-paid employees make in a month.

It has been said that all politics is local, but our local struggle in

North Carolina is of national significance because the extremist forces we have struggled against see our state as a testing ground for their plan to remake America not from DC down, but from the statehouse up. Without any sense of irony in places where "state sovereignty commissions" fought to maintain Jim Crow segregation laws fifty years ago, the American Legislative Exchange Council (ALEC) solicits donations on its website by asking people to help them "return sovereignty to the states." Under the leadership of the ALEC board member Thom Tillis, then speaker of the house in North Carolina, we saw what their plan looks like in action: the defunding of state government through a flat tax that increased the burden on poor people while giving the wealthiest a windfall; the denial of federally funded health care to half a million North Carolinians; the rejection of federal unemployment benefits for 170,000 individuals and their families; cuts to public education that increase teachers' workloads while decreasing overall compensation; deregulation of industries that have a demonstrated record of environmental abuse; a constitutional amendment to deny equal protection to gay and lesbian citizens; and the worst voter-suppression bill America has seen in over half a century. These were the ill-conceived and barely considered policy decisions about which we sought to instruct our legislators, as our state constitution guarantees every citizen the right to do. Rather than meet with us, Tillis and his colleagues had over a thousand of us, their constituents, illegally arrested, until a judge in Wake County Superior Court finally ruled in favor of our defense, nearly a year and a half after the first arrests. By that time, Thom Tillis was on his way to represent North Carolina in the US Senate.

As much as our Forward Together Moral Movement has sought to expose ALEC's state-based strategy to remake America, we have also tried to make clear to justice-loving people that any attempt to reconstruct America in these perilous times must likewise look to the states. And among these United States, our history of inequality and injustice is nowhere more rigidly defined and painfully exposed than in the

Southern states. But precisely for this reason, the South is also a deep well of resistance, struggle, and freedom movements. If we want to save the soul of America, we must look not only to states generally but to *Southern* states in particular. North Carolina is the one I know best.

Finally, I must say from the beginning that although this book is political, it is not simply that. As I've already noted, I am a preacher. In some progressive circles this makes me immediately suspect. Not long ago I was a guest on *Real Time with Bill Maher*, with one of America's most prominent atheists. Wearing my clerical collar, I realized that I stood out among his guests. So I decided to announce to Bill that I, too, am an atheist. He seemed taken aback, so I explained that if we were talking about the God who hates poor people, immigrants, and gay folks, I don't believe in that God either. Sometimes it helps to clarify our language.

As much as the human being is a political animal, I know that each of us is also a spiritual being. We have learned in our work in North Carolina that, whatever our religious traditions, we cannot come together to work for the common good by ignoring our deepest values. Rather, we grow stronger in our work together as we embrace those things we most deeply believe, standing together where our values unite us and learning to respect one another where our traditions differ. We cannot let narrow religious forces highjack our moral vocabulary, forces who speak loudly about things God says little about while saying so little about issues that are at the heart of all our religious traditions: truth, justice, love, and mercy. The movement we have witnessed—the movement we most need—is a moral movement.

I don't say this just because I believe it (though I do). I say it because I've seen it. Right here in North Carolina. Right here at home.

Ultimately, this is a book about how a moral movement can come home to where you are, exposing twenty-first-century injustice and giving us a shared vision for a Third Reconstruction to save the soul of America. Anything less, I fear, will mean the self-destruction of our nation. Amidst the din of those who incite old fears by saying it is time to "take back" America, a moral movement has arisen to insist that we must move forward together, not one step back. The Reconstruction we are engaged in aims for nothing less than liberty and justice for *all*. Whoever you are, this book is for you because it is the story of how, when we all get together, we can become something greater than the sum of our fears.

CHAPTER 1

Son of a Preacher Man

DURING THE CIVIL WAR, when the Southern states were determined to survive as a sovereign nation committed to keeping its slaves, General William T. Sherman led sixty thousand Union troops across the Mississippi River at Vicksburg, Mississippi, and up through the South on a long march that would finally end in central North Carolina. The last of General Joseph E. Johnston's Southern forces surrendered to Sherman at Bennett Place on April 26, 1865. While America's collective memory of Sherman's march is largely shaped by *Gone With the Wind*'s story of white people's loss, African American communities throughout the South remember how, wherever Sherman's troops established an encampment, that place became an island of freedom within the South. If you could get to one of those places, you didn't have to cross the Ohio River to gain your freedom. You were already free, right there at home.

Plymouth, North Carolina, was one such island, just twenty miles from a community that still bears the name Free Union. Because black people there had gained not only their freedom but also access to property and capital, the typical white power structure was not as rigid in and around Free Union. My father grew up there with an understanding that Native Americans, black folks, and white folks could share life together, even in the South. Though Jim Crow laws—laws in the South that, taken together, reinstated de jure racial segregation after Reconstruction—were on the books in North Carolina, "miscegenation" was evident in the faces of people my father knew growing up. I have uncles and cousins with eyes as blue as those of any white person you will ever meet. To survive in the 1940s and '50s, some of them went north and passed as white in places where no one knew their family history.

After receiving degrees in North Carolina and Georgia, my father went north to Indianapolis, where he studied at Butler University. He was a brilliant man, and he was encouraged by many of his teachers to continue in academic work. By the early 1960s he was a black man with two master's degrees, teaching in a Midwestern city with integrated schools. He met my mother there, and they married. Indianapolis was a place of opportunity for my father and our entire family.

But before I was old enough to start kindergarten, my parents received a call from E.V. Wilkins in North Carolina. An educator who had advocated for black children under segregation, Wilkins was also an activist who saw that change was coming to places like Plymouth. The National Association for the Advancement of Colored People (NAACP) in North Carolina had won some important victories for desegregation in the courts. But they needed educated black people on the ground to test the school systems' willingness to hire black teachers and enroll black students. Wilkins asked my father if he would come home and teach science in the public school. He agreed to do this. My mother took a job in the school office, and after a year in a segregated first-grade class, as a second-grader I was sent to integrate the all-white public school.

Nearly fifty years later, my mother still works for the Washington County Schools. The great-grandchildren of some people who called her nigger when we first came now call her Mama Barber. But my parents didn't have that kind of affirmation when they made the decision to come back and work for justice in eastern North Carolina. They came because they respected people like E.V. Wilkins, who were already deeply engaged in the work. And they came because they were called by God.

Because we came home to Roper, North Carolina, I grew up not only in my parents' home but also at my grandmamma's. My father's mother was, in so many ways, the spiritual anchor of our family. She had a way of watching over her children and grandchildren—of paying attention to the whole community—and seeing what was really going on. An elder in the traditional sense of our African and Native American ancestors, she kept the wisdom of those who had gone before her and passed it down to us, the next generation. I've had the privilege of being able to study at some of this country's best theological schools, and I have learned a great deal from professors of theology in those places. But everything I know that I know in a practical way—the faith that I hold most deeply—I learned from my grandmamma.

When we were growing up, Grandmamma and her nieces always cooked for the whole family (and for anyone else who happened to stop by). When I was at her house, I often sat with them in the kitchen. They would hum songs from church as she rolled out biscuits and stirred pots on her old gas stove. They also had a ritual whenever the food was done. Grandmamma would take a bottle of the anointing oil that she rubbed on people's heads when she prayed for them and slip it into the front of her apron. She and the other ladies would take some money, a rag, and some of the food they'd cooked and they would say, "We'll be back shortly. We've got to go and hope somebody."

As a young black boy learning proper English in school, I thought my uneducated grandmamma was misspeaking—that she mistook the word "hope" for "help." I even may have tried to correct her error in word choice a time or two. But looking back, I see that Grandmamma articulated more theology in that single phrase than some preachers manage to get into an entire sermon. As a person of faith struggling to survive in a society that so often despised her and the people she loved most, my grandmamma knew that any prayers worth their salt had to be accompanied by food for the hungry. She and other mothers of the church practiced "visitation" as a spiritual discipline, every bit as important as Sunday worship or Holy Communion. She knew in her bones that faith and works, belief and practice, were inseparable. And she knew in her careful choice of words that love in action was not simply about helping people. It was a practice of hope that both enabled others to keep going and helped her to keep her eyes on the prize and hold on.

Though she had no formal training in theology, my grandmamma knew what the great German theologian Jürgen Moltmann said so clearly: "Those who hope in Christ can no longer put up with reality as it is, but begin to suffer under it, to contradict it. Peace with God means conflict with the world, for the goad of the promised future stabs inexorably into the flesh of every unfulfilled present."[1] We become, as Dr. Cornel West says so well, not optimists who deny reality but prisoners of hope who work to change reality. I didn't know as a boy sitting at Grandmamma's kitchen table how important the faith she was showing me would be. But I took it all in just the same.

In time, I would come to see that the faith my grandmamma embodied was my father's primary motivation in life as well. William J. Barber, for whom I was named, was a Christian Church (Disciples of Christ) minister as long as I knew him. He was a powerful preacher who stood tall in the pulpit, proclaiming God's dream of freedom for captives to people who struggled daily against poverty, cultural trauma, and second-class citizenship. If he had gone to an urban center with more concentrated black wealth, he easily could have become a big-church preacher and lived the middle-class, professional lifestyle of his classmates from seminary. But coming home to Roper, North Carolina, was a vow of poverty for my father. He was not committed to professional advancement. He was devoted, instead, to the freedom of all people—especially those who have been overlooked by the powerful in society.

Though he was a fully credentialed preacher, my father was not employed as a pastor. He taught science at the local high school and did odd jobs in the community, providing for our family while, at the same time, building a broad network of connections in Washington County and throughout eastern North Carolina. Though no one used this language in rural North Carolina at the time, he was essentially a bivocational community organizer.

When we first came home to North Carolina, my parents began attending meetings at Elizabeth City State University, a historically black college. There they discussed with Mr. Wilkins, other leaders in the African American community, and some progressive whites the best strategy for a peaceful integration of Washington County's public schools. People were always coming by our house in the evenings to talk about issues. One man had a son who'd been wrongfully incarcerated on trumped-up charges. Another wanted to discuss labor rights at the local warehouse and how workers might organize for better wages and working conditions. Some neighbors were concerned about child care for working parents or establishing worker-owned co-ops to build economic power so they wouldn't be abused by the sharecropping system that had extended slavery's power dynamic into the twentieth century. My father could talk to all of them. He had the sort of quick, versatile mind that allowed him to sit down and work the New York Times crossword puzzle in twenty minutes, but he rode around in an old, beat-up pickup truck, looking like all the other farmhands in the area. Everyone who knew him called him Doc.

My father used to carry me to meetings when I was a little boy. Every once in a while someone would ask, "Why is this kid here?" And my father would always say, "Leave him alone. He's learning." I grew up in community meetings. Conversations that started when someone stopped by the house inevitably led to a community meeting where others with a similar concern would gather to discuss what could be done. These meetings happened in living rooms, in church basements, in Masonic lodges, and in barbershops. They were often small groups—ten or fifteen people getting together to talk. But my father took each individual seriously. No matter what the injustice, it mattered because people mattered. Every single one of them was created in the image of God. Like his mother, my grandmamma, my father was going to "hope" them any way he knew how.

But keeping faith alive in the 1960s Black Belt of North Carolina wasn't always easy. One of my earliest memories of childhood is of sitting on the floor of our living room in Roper. There is a little white TV set with tinfoil on the antenna, and my mother is sitting in front of that TV, bent over crying. For a long time, I didn't know what to make of that memory. But then I realized it must have been the spring of 1968. She was hearing for the first time about the death of Martin Luther King. In so many ways, her grief at the loss of the single African American freedom preacher who had risen to national prominence symbolizes for me the constant struggle that she and my father endured throughout their lives.

As Americans in the twenty-first century, it is easy for us to celebrate the MLK holiday or visit his national monument on the Mall in Washington, DC, without ever feeling the agony of the thousands of African Americans like my parents who struggled tirelessly for decades against the same forces that gunned down Dr. King. We can be inspired by King's dream without having to live through the nightmare of friends losing their land because they tried to register to vote or family members losing their jobs because they attended a union meeting. In my mind's eye I still see my mother bent over weeping. And I know that she was not only mourning the loss of Dr. King. She was mourning all the losses that she and my father had endured in the hope that, someday, justice would prevail and people who lived with their backs against the wall would indeed be free at last. When you've devoted your entire life to those people—when, in fact, you *are* those people—then the freedom movement is not a matter of history or social theory. It is a matter of life and death.

For my family, it was also always a matter of faith. I cannot remember a time when I did not know God both to be real and to be about bringing justice in this world. I've never experienced the epistemological crisis that is central to so many faith journeys in Western history, when individuals must learn to answer for themselves the question "How can I know that God is real?" But as a teenager I had to face a different kind of faith crisis. To so many of my fellow Americans, the God I knew was a stranger, the faith I was raised in, an anomaly. Before I could join the struggle that my parents had given their lives to, I had to wrestle with a church that seemed to hypocritically turn its back on them and the people they served.

I witnessed this hypocrisy firsthand as I observed my father's ministry. As a preacher without a congregation, my father often traveled, holding revivals in little country churches across eastern North Carolina. For him, this was always a twofold vocation. He was sharing the Gospel message that gave him hope, believing that it was good news for others as well. But at the same time he was also building connections as an organizer. As a sociologist, he thought about how the social institution of the church provided a network through which people could share information, organize around issues of common concern, and mobilize for collective action. As a people person, he knew that congregations answer a call to action not only because they believe it to be right but also because they know the pastor who is making the call. An organizer is always building relationships of trust. My father did this as a traveling evangelist.

But he knew well that not everyone in the Christian churches of eastern North Carolina believed, as he did, that God and justice always go hand in hand. As a historian my father wrote the book on the Christian Church (Disciples of Christ) in eastern North Carolina.[2] He traced how the Restorationist Movement, born of an integrated revival in early-nineteenth-century Kentucky, had evolved into the radical Christian notion that black and white could live, work, and worship together, even in the South. In North Carolina history, he observed how descendants of that revival—Christian church missionaries—were active participants in the post-Reconstruction Fusion Party, which united poor whites and freed slaves across North Carolina to stand together against the tyranny of white-supremacist Democrats in the late nineteenth century. Their challenge to white power was met by a racist propaganda campaign that resulted in America's only documented coup d'état, in Wilmington, North Carolina, in 1898. The grief I witnessed in my parents' experience of the death of Dr. Martin Luther King in

1968 was a reflection of the grief their forebears had borne seventy years earlier, when most of the black wealth in Wilmington was destroyed by white mobs who murdered dozens of African Americans, burned down the only African American daily newspaper in the country, and pillaged Wilmington's black-owned businesses district.[3]

My parents' was a grief that mourned the power death holds in this world, working through individuals and systems to crush human beings and their God-given potential. But it was more than that, I came to learn as I watched my father's relationship with the church. My father knew his history, so he was never surprised. He knew that fellow Christians had been deeply involved in justice work from Reconstruction on up until his time. But he also knew that Christians had been on the other side as well. Those same Christian Church (Disciples of Christ) churches of eastern North Carolina that had been so radically committed to a new world at their inception were often silent in the face of injustice. During the civil rights movement, when my father called these congregations to stand up for what was right, they often ignored him or said, "We can't move too quickly. All progress takes time."

Most popular understandings of the civil rights movement assume that black churches supported Dr. King because he was a minister, because mass meetings happened in church buildings, and because the moral language of the church was used in public appeals. But the fact is that there was no single "black church," just as there is no single white church—or no single America, for that matter. In his book *Prophesy Deliverance!*, the public intellectual and Union Theological Seminary professor Cornel West outlines five types of African American social engagement in response to modern racism. These different modes of existence, he acknowledges, were developed as people sought to survive in an economy built upon race-based slavery and white supremacy. Because of both a fear of reprisal for any challenge to the status quo and an internalized sense that "white was right," the "assimilationist" posture became a mode of survival for many black Christians who wanted life for their children to be a little bit easier than life had been for them.[4]

For these churches, "justice," was often a scary word. It invited the trouble they were intent on avoiding.

I did not have this framework for understanding the church as a boy, but I observed how often my father's ministry was marginalized by people who called themselves Christians. He was turned out of churches and ignored at denominational meetings and invitations to preach were canceled when someone said he was known to stir up trouble. To me, it seemed like the height of hypocrisy to chastise a fellow believer for taking the faith *too seriously*. As I said, I never doubted God, but I had serious reservations about the church. So the last thing I wanted to do was to become a preacher.

I thought I'd be a lawyer. My first year at North Carolina Central University, the nation's oldest public university for African Americans, I became the freshman class president. I majored in political science and began to explore notions of public justice as they are understood in sociological, economic, and political terms. My senior year, I got involved in organizing students. We marched to Raleigh to demand more funding for historically black colleges. After the fact, someone told me that it was the largest protest of university trustees on record in our state. Without knowing it, I was becoming an organizer. But I was also practicing the faith my grandmamma and my father had lived and preached.

When I was about to graduate, I got a call from Boston University. They offered me a scholarship to come and do graduate studies in theology. By this time, I knew Dr. King had gone to Boston University to do his doctoral studies before going to Montgomery, Alabama, where he met Rosa Parks and became a leader in the first intentionally nonviolent struggle for African American freedom. Learning about this man whose death had caused my mother such grief helped me to understand how faith and politics can go hand in hand, not only for individuals but for a social movement. I still didn't want to be a preacher, but I thought I might follow in Dr. King's footsteps as a human rights advocate and public intellectual.

So, I went home and told my grandmamma about the invitation to do graduate studies at Boston University. She immediately did something that always made me nervous. She got up, went to her bedroom, closed the door, and started to pray. You could hear her humming from outside the closed door. When she came out, she said, "Boy, you don't need to go to Boston."

I said to myself, "I love Grandmamma, but I'm not about to turn down a scholarship to graduate school." But a few weeks later, I realized I just couldn't go. I wanted to, but I couldn't. Something down deep inside of me was preventing me from going. I went to the president of my school and told him I was going to have to turn down Boston University.

I don't know what Grandmamma saw when she went into that room to pray, but I do know that three years later both she and my father were dead. I consider those two—my father and my grandmamma—to be the best friends I've ever had. And if I'd gone to Boston, I would have missed the last three years of their lives. I also got married in those years. My wife, Rebecca, had made it clear that she wasn't interested in a long-distance relationship. So I don't know if she would have waited on me.

I take seriously the Scripture that says, "In an abundance of counselors there is safety."[5] If it hadn't been for Grandmamma, who knew how to pray, I might have made a decision that wouldn't necessarily have been wrong, but would have changed my direction. I think about Paul in the New Testament and how he wanted to go to Spain but, as he wrote, "the Spirit prevented him." And it seems to me now that the Spirit must have kept me here in North Carolina. Somehow, Grandmamma knew that I couldn't just follow Dr. King's path. I had to find my own way.

Finding my way meant coming to terms with the faith my family had shown me—a prophetic Christianity that would connect me to a great river of resisters, stretching back to Ella Baker and Medgar Evers, to Harriet Tubman and Frederick Douglass, to John the Baptist and Mary of Bethany, to Queen Esther and the Hebrew prophet Micah, who asked in the eighth century BCE, "What doth the Lord require?" Dr. King had found his own place in this stream, as had my mother and father.

My vocation, I was learning, was to live an answer to this fundamental biblical question with my own life.

> He has showed you, O man, what is good;
> and what does the LORD require of you
> but to do justice, and to love kindness,
> and to walk humbly with your God?[6]

What never changes from age to age with God? What is always God's primary focus for His people? What transcends our labels, our political alliances, and our situational ethics? What is greater than the political majority at any given moment?

Do justice echoed in every ripple of the great river of resistance. Treat people right, treat communities right, treat the least of these right. *Love mercy*, I heard my faith tradition say. Love helping people. Love building a government that cares for all. Love the least, the left out, the lost. Enjoy lifting those who have been abandoned. Get excited about rescuing those who have failed. And this: *Walk humbly before your God*. Never think as a nation that your bombs, missiles, and weaponry make you greater than God. Never become a nation that's unable to repent when you have mistreated the vulnerable. Never become so arrogant in your wealth that you refuse to lift the poor. Never become so vain that you pray for God to bless America and forget that God is not your exclusive property.

Do justice. Love mercy. Walk humbly before your God.

Micah said it nearly three thousand years ago. And God's servants have been saying it ever since. Coming to terms with the church that seemed to turn its back on my father, I heard a call to take up Micah's message and reclaim moral language in the public square for the common good. The great river of resistance taught me that this is what God has always been about. And with God, some things never change.

Of course, this was the 1980s—the heyday for the Moral Majority and the ascendance of the Religious Right in America's public life. Neoconservatives were using biblical language to justify arms deals in Central America, a War on Drugs in America's cities, and the sellout of

government to private corporate interests. It was the worst of times for a
human rights advocate to discover himself to be a religious conservative
—for that's what I was, just not in the usual sense of the term. But
there I was. I could not deny that my deepest and truest beliefs were
those fundamental truths God had declared through Micah years ago.

I was not a politician. I wasn't a lobbyist. I wasn't going to be able to
give my life to a nonprofit that works for progressive ideals. Those people
and organizations do important work, but I had to find my own way.
God was calling me as a theological conservative to reclaim language
that had been hijacked by those who liberally resist and ignore so much
of God's character.

Of course, these theological conservatives' rationale was not new.
During slavery many so-called conservative Christians claimed deep ad-
herence to Scripture in their support of slavery and racism. They pulled
out a few texts to build a whole system of injustice, while ignoring the
multiplicity of texts that condemned human oppression. Though claiming to be biblicists, they overlooked as much of the Bible as they could,
pretending that a half reading of a few selected texts justified slavery over
and against the heart of God's long work to free creation from bondage.

During the civil rights movement there were many who found ways
to dismiss the biblical call for justice and righteousness. Many of them
were so liberal in their dispelling of God's demands that they criticized
Dr. King, saying that he was not "acting like a preacher." He had to re-
mind them that if you read and accept the whole counsel of the triune
God, then you must challenge the threefold evils of racism, classism,
and militarism in our society. Like my father, Dr. King simply insisted
that with God, some things never change. The more I paid attention to
our tradition, the more urgently I heard the call to conserve its heart
of liberation from the liberal dismissal of moral truth for the sake of
individual gain.

I came to see that in our shifting times, as so many were trying to
promote the benign and anemic Christianity that reduces the image of
God to a mere sanctifier of our nation, I was called to preach. It seemed

as if I heard God's voice saying, "Come out of the exile of false religion. Come out of the exile of the religion of idolatry and self-worship, which can only sustain oppression. Come out of the exile of religion that serves itself and avoids real people, the vulnerable people whom God adores. Come out of the religion that has liberally removed itself from the unchanging values of God and dared to call itself conservative."

Maybe I had resisted the call because I knew from watching my parents what it would cost. But they had baptized me in the river of resistance, saturating my mind with freedom songs that would not go away. Grandmamma was praying for me long before she went into her bedroom that day and closed the door. She was praying with every song she hummed, in every plate of food she carried out to hope somebody. Though she had crossed over to the other side of the river, I knew she was praying still.

I didn't know just how soon I'd be crying out to God for myself.

$200.00

A A P $ 256.
          $1056. 00
    E Progressive

CHAPTER 2

My First Fight

BY THE TIME I graduated from seminary in 1989, my grandmamma and my father were dead. But their faith was like a seed planted inside me. The Reverend Dr. William C. Turner, who had become a spiritual father after I lost my two best friends during my studies at Duke Divinity School, preached my installation service when I received a call to pastor Fayette Street Christian Church, across North Carolina's northern border, in Martinsville, Virginia. People my grandmamma's age started calling me Reverend Barber when I was twenty-six.

I'll never forget my initial sermon at Fayette Street. As a young preacher in a new setting, I had prepared carefully, rehearsing my message and perfecting its delivery. Before I left home to drive to the church, I packed my ministerial robes and a new pair of dress shoes I'd purchased for this occasion. Like a groom on his wedding day, I wanted to look my best. But when unloading the car at the church, I realized that my shoes were missing. I had no choice but to don my robe and walk into the pulpit in the tennis shoes I was wearing. When the service was over, one of the mothers of the church pulled me aside and said, "Son, if you can preach like that in tennis shoes, you keep on wearin' 'em." The next week, she brought me a little key chain with tennis shoes on it.

So I set about doing the work of a pastor. I visited my people in their homes and prepared sermons in my study. I worked on the craft of preaching even as I tried to pay attention to what was happening in people's lives and in the life of that small town. Nestled in the foothills of the Blue Ridge Mountains, Martinsville could have appeared to a nostalgic observer as a Mayberry where everyone knew one another and took care of their own. But it did not take long to discover the fault lines that ran deep beneath the picturesque veneer of this small Southern town.

My first New Year's Day in Martinsville, the black churches in town invited me to preach the annual Emancipation Day service. A celebration of President Lincoln's executive action to free slaves, in 1863, Emancipation Day services are a century-and-a-half-old tradition in the black freedom movement. It was a heady time for a young freedom preacher. Nelson Mandela had been released from Robben Island in South Africa just months earlier, and Doug Wilder had just been elected the first African American governor of Virginia—indeed, the first black governor of any US state since Reconstruction. My wife and I were living in the church parsonage, where, we learned, the first savings and loan for African Americans in Martinsville had been started in the attic, just after the Civil War. Across the street from the church was the site of the old school that had afforded African Americans an education since the great jubilee of 1863.

It was easy to be hopeful in my Emancipation Day sermon in southern Virginia that first day of January, 1990. My enthusiasm about the power of God to break chains and set captives free stirred the spirits of some workers who had been trying to organize a union at the local textile factory. They came to me and told me that, for each year of service to the company, a factory worker only earned three dollars toward retirement. So, folks who had given their lives to that company for thirty years were being sent home with ninety dollars and a company watch. What's more, they had begun to realize that the chemicals they had worked with for decades had drastically increased their chances of developing cancer. A woman in my congregation retired only to discover that her cancer was already advanced to a degree that it could not be treated. I sat with her family and watched her die in poverty from a disease she had contracted while working for the factory.

Now, after hearing my Emancipation Day message, workers from that same factory were asking me to help them start a union. I was not a very experienced pastor, but I knew that I could not pretend to love a family I had grieved with if I was not willing to take a stand against the systemic injustice that had taken their mother from them. In essence, I had no choice. If I were going to do this work of pastoring, I had to join the fight.

No sooner than I had begun to support the union effort in Martinsville, I started receiving calls and visits from movement people—many of them old friends of my father. All of them were elders whom I respected and whose analysis I considered carefully. But they were not of one mind. Some supported the union, insisting that civil rights and worker's rights must go hand in hand because racism and poverty have always been inextricably bound together in the South. Others insisted that I should not support the union because good factory jobs were fading away quickly with no clear replacement to follow them in small Southern towns. Corporate bosses who were pressured too hard by unions would close up shop and move elsewhere, leaving their former workers unemployed and impoverishing towns like Martinsville. Sure, wages weren't all we might hope for, they said. But they were better than nothing.

Listening to the analysis of both sides, my mind had to acknowledge the legitimate concerns and at least partial truths of each party. Martinsville had indeed suffered from the divide-and-conquer strategy of post–civil rights deconstruction. The pro-union activists were right to insist in the wake of Doug Wilder's fusion coalition victory that we must pursue a pro-labor, white-and-black-together strategy. But, at the same time, ongoing viable businesses in the community were essential to everyone's well-being. The factory owners could not simply be our enemy. The community needed them as much as they needed us.

As I studied and listened, I learned how essential an economic and political analysis is to moral leadership. Not only must we know the arguments on all sides of any debate, we must also seriously consider the questions that are not being asked and their implications for everyone involved. My very first fight in Martinsville, Virginia, etched this principle of moral leadership deep in my soul: *Before you get loud, be sure you're not wrong.*

But I was also learning how the essential work of careful reasoning on any social issue can lead to a "paralysis of analysis." People who mean well in both the church and community often hear arguments on each side of an issue, throw up their hands, and say, "It's complicated. There are good people on both sides."

They are right, of course. But I could not forget the family of that woman who had died of cancer, seemingly helpless in the face of overwhelming powers. An economic and political analysis helped me to see more clearly the multiple factors that contributed to her suffering. But only a moral analysis offered the clarity that would compel us to do something. We weren't trying to start a union simply because it was the smartest or most politically advantageous thing to do. We were going to start a union because it was the *right* thing to do.

As a preacher, I assumed that my greatest allies in moral leadership would be fellow clergy in town. So I was encouraged when we heard that the president of the textile factory was willing to host a clergy breakfast at his corporate office. When I arrived I was impressed by the number of ministers present, many of them already enjoying the good food that had been spread out on nicely decorated tables. I joined them, eager to talk about our strategy before the president arrived. But shortly after I took my seat, the president stepped in, shaking hands and calling each minister by name. "Good to see you, Reverend Johnson. How's that parking lot we paved for you working out? Hello, Reverend Smith. How was your anniversary service? Sorry I couldn't make it."

He made his way around the room, shaking hands and reminding all the ministers of the ways he'd been a benefactor to them and their congregations. Without ever taking a seat, he finished his round of greetings, then stood at the head of the table, thanking us for our good work in the community. As he was telling us what else he had to do that morning and starting to say his goodbyes, I raised my hand and said, "Mr. President, I thought we were meeting this morning to talk about the union."

With a smile, he looked at me and said, "We just did." A couple of days later, I read a letter in the newspaper, signed by most of the ministers who had attended that breakfast. In the most thoughtful and compassionate language possible, it explained why, as a group, they could not support the union.

With that, our union movement was finished. The Bible says Judas betrayed Jesus for forty pieces of silver. But the moral leadership of Martinsville sold out for much less. A nice breakfast and a few friendly reminders of who was in charge were enough to squelch the moral dissent of our group. Disappointed, I sat in my study, trying to understand how this had happened and where our efforts had gone wrong. I found myself praying with the psalmist, "O LORD, how long shall the wicked, how long shall the wicked triumph?"

Though I knew we had lost the fight, I couldn't shake the moral analysis that remained so clear. There it was in the prayer book I had been given by generations of Jews and Christians before me as a guide for leading God's people in worship.

> They crush thy people, O LORD,
> and afflict thy heritage.
> They slay the widow and the sojourner,
> and murder the fatherless;
> and they say, "The LORD does not see;
> the God of Jacob does not perceive."[1]

I had studied political science in college and had, at the invitation of a friend, worked on a lieutenant governor's campaign during graduate school. I knew enough about realpolitik to understand that we didn't have a power base to move a union campaign forward in Martinsville. I had also read in seminary the work of the great twentieth-century social ethicist Reinhold Niebuhr, whose concept of Christian realism suggested that faith-based notions of justice and mercy could motivate "moral man" to engage political issues. But Niebuhr had cautioned that "immoral society" would always require those seeking justice in this world to compromise and calculate their political effectiveness. Yes, a moral analysis might get preachers engaged in a campaign for a union, Christian realism said. But effective work for justice in the real world would require real political power. It wasn't enough to stand up for what was right. Before you stand, you also need to know who has your back.[2]

Niebuhr's critique of a simplistic moral analysis forced me to think practically about strategy. I had to admit that I had been naïve going into my first fight. I was pastoring some of the workers who were directly affected, and I knew why I was compelled to support them. I had listened to arguments for and against a union by people I respected. But that was all. I had falsely assumed that the moral authority of preachers would be enough to sway a corporate boss in a small Southern town. I had not thought to ask who would stand with us in the fight.

But even as I was learning from the analysis of Christian realism, I also knew that I could not trust its basic assumption that faithful action is determined by political effectiveness. I could admit that we had lost, and I wanted to learn from my mistakes. But I also knew that standing for the union had been the right thing to do.

I needed something more than Christian realism to guide me in the task of leading people who had lost a fight but still knew that the Lord was on their side. Thankfully, I had the time-tested prayer book of the Hebrew children that had been written down in exile, centuries after God had brought Israel up out of Egypt. The words of Psalm 94 kept resounding in my ears: "Who rises up for me against the wicked? Who stands up for me against evildoers?"[3]

Psalm 94 insisted that moral dissent is still necessary even when there is no reasonable expectation of political success. When we stand for right, even if we feel that we are standing by ourselves, we are in good company. When we raise a voice of moral dissent, we don't only stand with Moses against Pharaoh. We also stand with William Lloyd Garrison, the nineteenth-century abolitionist who denounced slavery when its abolition was a political impossibility. When the mayor of Boston had him jailed, supposedly for his own safety, Garrison wrote these words on the wall of his cell: "William Lloyd Garrison was put into this cell on Wednesday afternoon, Oct. 21, 1835, to save him from the violence of a 'respectable' and influential mob, who sought to destroy him for preaching the abominable and dangerous doctrine that 'all men are created equal' and that all oppression is odious in the sight of God."[4]

The nineteenth-century abolitionists didn't stand up against slavery because they knew they had the numbers to defeat it. They stood up and raised their voices in moral dissent because they knew that slavery was wrong. Likewise, in 1846, when Mexican forces fired upon US troops who had been sent across a disputed border to provoke just such an incident, President James K. Polk asked Congress for a declaration of war because "American blood had been shed on American soil." But a freshman Congressman from Illinois who did not know that it wasn't his place to raise a moral dissent introduced the "Spot Resolution," which would have required President Polk to identify the exact spot on US soil where the attack had occurred. The resolution was defeated, and many seriously questioned Congressman Abraham Lincoln's patriotism for introducing it. But nearly two decades before his second inaugural address, Lincoln had stood up in Congress to raise a moral dissent.

Henry David Thoreau, too, stood against the Mexican-American War in the mid-nineteenth century, refusing to pay a poll tax that would support imperialism and the expansion of race-based slavery into Mexican territory. Though he was arrested, Thoreau wrote in his classic work "Civil Disobedience" that it is the duty of everyone to disobey any law they find morally objectionable. This had been, he argued, the very basis of the American Revolution. But when Thoreau's friend Ralph Waldo Emerson visited him in jail, Emerson was taken aback at his friend's moral dissent.

"Henry," Emerson reportedly asked through the jail cell's bars, "What are you doing *in there?*"

To which Thoreau replied, "Ralph, what are you doing *out there?*"

In the American struggle for justice and freedom, moral dissent has always seemed impractical when it began. Yet people of conviction have responded to the psalmist's basic question by answering, "Here I am. Send me." In 1896, when the US Supreme Court upheld the constitutionality of "separate but equal" in the case of *Plessy v. Ferguson*, Justice John Marshall Harlan of Kentucky stood alone to write a dissenting opinion. By any political calculation at that moment, his words were simply a waste of time. But looking back, we can see that every legal challenge to segregation in the twentieth century was based upon the careful reasoning of Justice Harlan, whom history would name the Great Dissenter. Without his words, NAACP attorneys could not have successfully argued for the desegregation of public schools nearly six decades later in *Brown v. Board of Education*. Justice Harlan lost by a landslide in 1896. But he won history.

As I contemplated the necessity of moral dissent with Psalm 94 open before me, I looked up the street from the church parsonage at the little school where the black children of Martinsville had been educated through the late nineteenth and early twentieth centuries. Many of the elders in my congregation had attended that school. Whether they knew Justice Harlan's words or not, their existence was a living sign that the Great Dissenter had not stood alone when he insisted that separate could not be equal. Teachers had sacrificed to ensure a quality education for black children. The community had organized to construct and maintain a building when public funds were severely limited. People of faith had gathered on Sunday mornings and at midweek prayer services for decades to cry out to God and to teach their children, "Red and yellow, black and white, *all* are precious in God's sight."

The psalmist was right: "If the LORD had not been my help, my soul would soon have dwelt in the land of silence."[5] Where political realism would have silenced dissent, faith had made it possible for a moral voice to cry aloud and spare not. But the faith that inspired moral dissent was not blind faith. It was, rather, conviction that took the long view. Even when they could not see now how justice would prevail, generations of dissenters knew that it would. Even when they felt alone in the moment, they knew they were part of a "great cloud of witnesses" in the long movement toward justice.

I thought I had come to Martinsville to practice preaching—to get some on-the-job experience as a pastor. But it turned out that the lived experience of a community of moral dissent converted me to the faith that my grandmamma and my father had shown me. It had been one of the great privileges of my life to have those two saints always praying over me and speaking into my life. But now I was in a new place, and they were not there to speak directly to me. I did, however, have the same prayer book that had guided them. In the wake of my first real experience of defeat, the Psalter was teaching me to pray. In words that had sustained generations of moral dissent, I came to know the liberating God of history for myself.

As I wrestled intellectually with the fundamental shortcoming of Christian realism, I recalled that Reinhold Niebuhr's social concern had also grown out of his experience pastoring in early-twentieth-century Detroit. Niebuhr had witnessed the great northern migration of a generation of Southern sharecroppers who left the confines of Jim Crow racism for the hope of opportunity in Henry Ford's automobile factories. Observing the imbalance of power between corporate bosses and factory workers, Niebuhr had also sided with the unions. But as a German American whose whiteness afforded him access to the dominant religious culture, Niebuhr did not stay with the black and poor white workers of Detroit to develop his concept of Christian realism. Instead, he moved to Union Theological Seminary in New York City and tried to apply the principles of established religion to the struggles of oppressed people through the teaching of "practical theology." Even though Niebuhr had sought to develop Christian realism in the service of people like the factory workers of Martinsville, it seemed to me that he had missed their essential theological contribution to any theory of Christian social engagement. "If God be for you," the saints at Fayette Street asked, "who can be against you?" A faith that had been born under and sustained over and against injustice knew implicitly the abso-lute necessity of moral dissent.

We lost that first fight in Martinsville, but it was an invaluable ex-perience for me. The language of faith was not simply, as I had seen in seminary, a medium that had to be reclaimed from the reactionary ex-tremists of the Moral Majority and the so-called religious right. Nor was it merely a catalyst to compel individuals to engage with immoral soci-ety within the framework of Christian realism. No, the liberating faith of the Psalter gave me an agenda for moral dissent. Preaching the proph-ets reminded me that moral dissent is nothing new; we have a goodly heritage. And teaching Jesus as a practitioner of moral dissent helped me to identify strategies and tactics to sustain people in their struggle, both in and beyond the church. Though I had not found a name for it yet, my first fight in Martinsville was forcing me to develop a new imagination for social engagement that was built upon a fundamental commitment to the necessity of moral dissent.

The New Testament Letter to the Hebrews offered an apt summary statement for the posture required by the faith I was learning: "But we are not of those who shrink back and are destroyed, but of those who believe and are saved."[6] In a movement based upon moral dissent, defeat does not cause us to doubt our purpose or question the ends toward which we strive. We do not belong to those who shrink back, for we know the tragic truth of history. When oppressed people shrink back, they will always be forgotten and destroyed. Faith-rooted moral dissent requires that we always look forward toward the vision of what we know we were made to be. But defeat can and must invite us to question our means. While realism cannot determine the goals of our faith, it must shape our strategy in movements of moral dissent.

Right there in Martinsville, I began to look long and hard at the mistakes of our efforts rooted in moral dissent. One of the first things I realized was that we had not applied the insight of civil rights veterans who had affirmed our support for the union. Their historical analysis suggested that a black preacher ought to support the union because powerful white people would always strive to "divide and conquer" poor folks. If white workers could be persuaded not to trust black workers, then they would vote against their own economic interests. Although I had found the argument persuasive, I had not gotten to know any of the white workers in the union movement. I recalled the minister's breakfast with the factory president. It had seemed normal at the time, but looking back, I realized that only black pastors had been there. The company president must have met separately with the white pastors, and we had no idea what he had said to them. It was now clear to me that we had been vulnerable to defeat because we allowed ourselves to be divided.

I had found Niebuhr's Christian realism insufficient because of the blind spot his white privilege created. But when I turned the search light of truth onto my own soul, I had to acknowledge my own assumptions and fears. I remembered an evening in 1975, when I was twelve years old, visiting the home of my uncle who had married a white woman in eastern North Carolina. In the darkness of that night, we looked out the window of their home to see a fiery cross illuminating a small crowd of men. With an almost eerie sense of calm, my uncle took a shotgun off its rack, handed it to me, and said, "Stand by the back door and shoot anything that moves."

My family knew that we had the blood of black, white, and Native American ancestors flowing in our veins. I was never opposed to integration on principle. But I learned firsthand to fear white anger and the violence of white mobs. For me, a twelve-year-old boy, it had been a matter of life and death.

Fifteen years later, those patterns of mistrust and suspicion that had been written upon my young soul were being used by people in power to subvert my work for human freedom. I naturally trusted the black workers and their pastors. But I was suspicious of white workers and their allies. I had good personal reasons for these inclinations, just as others had reason to trust their own gut. But Martinsville showed me that Jesus's insistence that we love our enemies is more than an ethical ideal. In the struggle for human freedom, it is also a practical necessity. If love does not drive out the fears that so easily divide us, we will never gather together in coalitions strong enough to challenge those who benefit from injustice.

"Power concedes nothing without a demand," Frederick Douglass said during the nineteenth-century abolition struggle, articulating a reality that no black person in America has ever been able to ignore. But Douglass also experienced the ability of a movement that builds wide and deep to sustain a moral fight until it is won. Douglass gained his personal freedom on his own, but he knew he would have to work with others to free the enslaved black people of America. He worked with Garrison and with the Grimke sisters, Angelina and Sarah, abolitionists from South Carolina. He worked with Sojourner Truth and Harriet Tubman. He worked with Quakers and evangelicals, with British sympathizers and with radicals like John Brown. Douglass knew what I was now learning: in the struggle for justice, we always need all the friends we can get.

I was grateful for my friendship with Chevis Horne, a white pastor in Martinsville who stood with us in our struggle for justice even when many of the black pastors were willing to sign the statement against the union. Horne knew the importance of friendships across the color line. The foreword to one of his books was written by Gardner C. Taylor, a friend and confidant of Dr. King's who founded the National Progressive Baptist Convention.

Not long after we lost the union fight in Martinsville, a young white woman named Michelle came to see me. She introduced herself as a daughter of the family that owned one of the big furniture companies there in town. I didn't know what she wanted to talk about, but I was immediately suspicious. *Why does she want to talk to me?*

It turned out that she had heard about the union fight and our moral concern had resonated with her. She wanted to talk because she, too, had a moral concern. Michelle had grown up listening to local businessmen talk at her family's dinner table. She knew how things worked in Martinsville. But she had recently learned that toxic chemicals were being stored in a black neighborhood without any neighbors' knowledge. She knew it was wrong, and she wanted me to help her stop it.

I agreed to help Michelle investigate the situation. We did our homework, staking out the place at night and photographing the warning labels on the trucks that were unloaded. It turned out she was right: not only were extremely toxic materials being stored there but also leaky barrels were being left to drain into the ground. Michelle and I worked together to form a little organization that we called Sensible Concerns About Toxins (SCAT). We were careful to make sure the leadership of this group included black and white, poor and well-to-do citizens of Martinsville. We moved from our research to an education phase, using public meetings, press conferences, and marches to get the word out. When someone would tell us, "We're with you, but we can't march," we'd say, "That's OK. You know people. Tell them what's going on."

The owners of the property argued that they were doing nothing wrong. It was their land, they said; they could do what they wanted with it. But by the time they started fighting back, we had a coalition broad enough that no single business interest could beat it. Our spokesperson, Ms. Gloria Hilton, was a woman from the neighborhood who had taught public school in the community for over thirty years. When she spoke, people listened. And her moral authority was backed up by people who looked like her and people who didn't. We were a force that the old guard of Martinsville had not imagined having to reckon with, but we were a force more powerful than even we could fully see.

Before SCAT's work was completed, my wife's mother got sick and our family decided to help care for her. I wasn't there to celebrate the final victory with our allies, but I stayed in touch and saw for myself the single-family homes that were built on that property for low-income families after the storage area had been removed and the soil cleaned up. More than twenty years later, Ms. Hilton still lives in that neighborhood.

She says the coalition that came together there in the early nineties not only reclaimed a piece of land that was being abused, it also gave the neighborhood a focal point of pride.

For me, my three years in Martinsville were the crash course in moral leadership that I didn't know I needed. Our defeat in the union struggle sent me to my prayer closet and taught me how moral dissent is central to my vocation as pastor. But it also helped me imagine the kind of coalition politics that we were able to practice in a local campaign against environmental racism. I came back to North Carolina knowing both the fights I couldn't run away from and something about what it would take to win them. Only a fusion coalition representing all the people in any place could push a moral agenda over and against the interests of the powerful. But such coalitions are never possible without radical patience and stubborn persistence. I was about to learn both in a struggle I would never have chosen.

CHAPTER 3

Learning to Stand Together

I LEARNED A GREAT DEAL in Martinsville about moral leadership—more than I realized at the time. But I did not know what was next for me when our family moved back to North Carolina in 1991. Preaching had helped me find a voice of moral dissent, but my father had shown me long before that you don't have to pastor a church to preach. I was at the core of my being a preacher, but I knew that preaching did not have to be my job. In fact, I had begun to think I might be more effective if it weren't. The pastoral work of managing a tight-knit community was not without its challenges and frustrations, which inevitably took time and energy away from public justice work. One of my aunts kept telling me I needed to stop trying to be a lawyer. I wasn't sure what I was trying to become, but I knew I wasn't in a hurry to find another church.

At the invitation of some friends, I preached at a youth event in the eastern part of the state. After the program ended that evening, Andrea Harris introduced herself to me as an old friend of my father's. She asked what I was doing, and I told her I wasn't sure yet. "Why don't you come work for me?" she asked.

Andrea had started the North Carolina Institute for Minority Economic Development to combat wealth inequality, which she knew to be rooted in America's history of slavery. She understood the work of creating business opportunities for people of color as freedom work. I went to work for Andrea and learned about strategies for economic empowerment and business development. But after just a few months on the job, I got a call from Carolyn Coleman.

Ms. Coleman explained to me that Mr. E.V. Wilkins—the same man who had called my father back to North Carolina a quarter century earlier—had recommended me to chair Governor Jim Hunt's Human Relations Commission. I accepted the appointment and began a crash course in the inner workings of state government. I traveled North Carolina from "Manteo to Murphy," as we say, following up on concerns about employment discrimination and fair housing. I got to know firsthand the history of hate groups in our state and the ways they continued to intimidate minorities, especially in rural communities. One of the first cases I investigated—and the first one we won—was that of a white woman who was refused housing by a landlord because of her friendship with black people. I got the first death threat of my life on that job. It was, in many ways, a trial by fire.

But working with the Human Relations Commission helped me to learn something important about the work I'm called to do. It did not matter whether I was someone's pastor or their representative to the governor; whatever my role, I heard the same cry. Vulnerable people could be ignored, used, pushed to the side, or intimidated. Still, something in their humanity cried out for justice. And I could not ignore it. However I made a living, I knew I would make a life as my grandmamma and my father had before me here in North Carolina. By my late twenties, my vocation was clear: I was called to stand for justice.

Meanwhile, churches kept calling me to preach. In the summer of 1993, I got a call from Greenleaf Christian Church, a small congregation in my denomination down in Goldsboro, North Carolina. I was traveling regularly for my state work at the time, but we were living an hour away from Goldsboro in Durham, where my wife worked as a nurse at the hospital. Greenleaf was looking for a pastor, but I told them I wasn't interested. I had a job I was happy with. I said I would be glad to come down and preach one Sunday while they looked for someone else, but they didn't need to evaluate me as a candidate. I was just there to preach. After I preached my first service at Greenleaf, one of the old mothers of the church came up and said, "Boy, you need to hush 'cause that's not what the Lord says. You need to come down here and be our pastor."

I resisted. Durham is centrally located in North Carolina, and our place there seemed to make sense. We were raising a young family as two working parents, trying to make ends meet and keep everyone's schedules together. It didn't feel like a time to uproot. It also didn't make any sense to leave a city for an impoverished community down east where we didn't really know anyone. I had a good job that paid me to do the work I felt called to do. I tried to just smile at the church ladies and say, "Don't ya'll worry. God will send you the right pastor." But it turned out they were right. The pastor God was sending them was me. In mid-July of that summer, I told Greenleaf that it didn't make any sense to me, but I was going to yield to the Spirit and test the Lord's leading for a few months as their pastor.

A fortnight later, on the first Friday in August, I woke up at home and could not move. At first, it was hard for me to even conceive of what was happening. I tried to bend my knees, but nothing happened. I thought I'd roll over, but I couldn't lift either side of my body off the bed. When I tried to lift my leg, it lay on the bed like a dead weight. I called out to my wife, bewildered by my sudden immobility.

An ambulance came and drove me to the hospital, where I would spend the next three months. Immediately the doctors starting doing scans and running tests, but no one could explain what was happening. All of my life I had been active. I played football in high school, stayed on my feet day and night through college, and lived life on the go as a pastor and chair of the Human Relations Commission. But lying on my back in that hospital bed, I turned thirty thinking I might never walk again.

Eventually I was diagnosed with a tremendous case of ankylosing spondylitis, an extreme form of arthritis that fuses your bones in place. My neck, the base of my spine, and my hips had all locked up simultaneously. There was no cure for this condition, but the doctors said that I might regain some mobility with intensive physical therapy. They started wheeling me down to the gym every day, but it felt like a knife was stabbing me in the hip whenever they bent my legs.

I took a lot of pain meds during those months. I hurt so bad when I was in the hospital that if someone had come in there and told me they had something that would make it all go away, I don't know if I could have said no. It was just that bad. I often tell people this is why I have compassion for folks who are hooked on drugs. It's hard to explain the despair that intense chronic pain can cause, making it impossible to think of anything else. I slipped into a depression and spent many long nights just crying in my bed.

But all through that time, people from the church kept visiting during the day. I could hardly talk to them, but they would say, "We want you to come back." I'd say, "Look at me. I can't come back as a cripple." But they would say, "We think you have something to offer. Just hold on."

That was a time in my life when it felt like something bad happened every summer. My father had died in the summer. Rebecca's mother died in the summer. Our young daughter had to have brain surgery one summer. The next summer, our son had a vitamin deficiency problem. Then this: at the end of that summer, I was told I'd never walk again. I appreciated the encouragement from the church and my family, but I simply couldn't believe that things would get better. The pain was too much to ignore. The thought of living the rest of my life that way was too much to bear. I didn't have it in me to keep going.

One night as I lay moaning under the weight of despair, a lady I didn't know came into my room in a wheelchair. She said, "I heard you were in here. I've come to pray for you." I said, "Ma'am, I really don't want to talk to you right now." But she said, "Well, you can't get out of bed. So I'm gonna talk, and you gonna listen."

She said to me, "Look, they've taken both my legs off. Now I'm goin' on home to get me some new legs, but God's not through with you yet. You remember that: you've got some work left to do." She bowed her head and prayed for me, even though I wouldn't reach out and hold her hand. When she had finished praying, she said goodbye and wheeled herself out of the room.

The next morning I called the nurse in and asked her if she could get my mother to come play some hymns on the piano in the hospital lobby. I said, "If I can get down there and sing with her, I think I can get myself together." Then I said, "I'd also like to get that double amputee who was in here last night to come down with me." But the nurse looked at me and said, "We don't have an amputee on this floor." I said, "Yes you do. She came in here last night and prayed for me." But nobody ever could find that woman. I call her my amputee angel.

After that experience, I started to get up out of my hospital bed. I still had a lot of pain, but I wasn't trying to do it alone anymore. My angel had called me out of myself, and I started to learn how to live with help from others. My therapists helped me learn how to get up on a walker, and my wife and my kids helped me around the house. All the while, the church told me, "We can figure out how to make this work, pastor." They sent drivers to pick me up and I went in and out of every pulpit I preached from on a walker.

I would go places on my walker and people in the audience would look around and ask, "When is the speaker coming?" They just assumed a guy in my shape couldn't be the preacher. But I started getting letters from folks who heard me preach. They would say, "Our marriage was about to fall apart, but when we saw you press your way on that walker, we said, 'We can make this marriage work.'"

I started my ministry at Greenleaf on that walker. We moved to Goldsboro and planted ourselves in that community, knowing that I couldn't even care for myself without help. People kept saying to me, "You can't do all this. You're going to kill yourself." But I just said, "I know I can't do it. But we can build community to do this. I don't need to do it if we can get together."

When I look at the Scriptures, it seems like everybody God chose to use had some major disfigurement or disability. Isaiah describes the "suffering servant." Moses, whom God called to be the spokesperson for Israel at Pharaoh's court, said he couldn't speak without stuttering. Paul the Apostle writes about a "thorn in his flesh"—something he just couldn't shake. But somehow, Paul wrote, God's "power is made perfect in weakness."[1] When I started pastoring at Greenleaf, I would walk to the pulpit on my walker, then swing it around behind me while I preached. That went on for twelve years. Whenever I was in the pulpit, I never felt the pain.

Looking back, I see now that I was learning how to stand through those years. I was learning firsthand the power of standing together.

I had long known the power of standing together biblically. When Moses, Aaron, and that rod came together, Pharaoh came down and the Red Sea opened up. When Esther and her uncle Mordecai came together, they were able to stop the plots of destruction against the Jewish people. When David, his slingshot, and his faith came together on the battlefield, Goliath fell. And I read somewhere that the headline in the *Jerusalem Morning Herald* the next day was "The bigger they come, the harder they fall!"

As a preacher, I knew what coming together could do biblically. And as an inheritor of the Southern freedom movement, I also knew what it had done historically. My father made sure I knew that justice had never lost when people came together in fusion coalitions. He never said justice wasn't fought. He didn't say it wasn't beat down. But when people come together, he told me, justice has never lost.

During slavery it looked like justice had lost, but when Harriet Tubman and Frederick Douglass and some Quakers and white evangelicals got together, they formed a fusion movement that brought about abolition. There was a time when women didn't have the right to vote. But when Sojourner Truth and Elizabeth Cady Stanton got together, they won the franchise. *Plessy v. Ferguson* looked like it had the victory, but when Thurgood Marshall got white lawyers and black lawyers and Jewish lawyers together, an all-white Supreme Court with one member who'd been part of the Ku Klux Klan voted unanimously to tear down "separate but equal." In the mid-twentieth century, it looked like the system of Jim Crow had built a fortress around segregation in the South; but when Rosa Parks and Martin Luther King and Bayard Rustin got together with Glen Smiley and Abraham Joshua Heschel and Viola Liuzzo, they tore down segregation and showed America a better way.

History showed me that what the Bible says is true: when we all get together, something powerful can happen. But what I knew biblically and historically took on a whole new depth of meaning when I experienced it personally. Alone on my sickbed, I had nearly given up on life and the work that God had called me to do. By myself, I simply couldn't imagine a way forward. But something happened when I got together in prayer with my amputee angel. Some new strength showed up when my mother and I got together at that piano. Then my doctors and my nutritionist got together. My swim coach and my therapists got together. My family and my church got together, and we learned the truth of that old hymn which says, "When we all get together / what a day of rejoicing that will be!"

It didn't happen all at once. I was on that walker for twelve years, but some lessons in life are so important that you can't learn them in a semester and put them down on a final exam. Some lessons are so important you have to get them down into your bones. I think that's what was happening to me all those years. I was learning the awesome power of what happens when people come together. And I was learning it in the church.

Greanleaf was a small congregation in a small military town. In so many ways, it was the sort of tight-knit community of people with long histories that I had been trying to get away from. But accepting the call to become their pastor as I was beginning the greatest personal struggle of my life, I saw how much I needed them. God had called us together to do something and to become something that none of us could do or be on our own. Dealing with the personal needs and individual struggles of our members was not a distraction from justice work, I came to see; it was, instead, an invitation to learn from experience what God's justice looks like in this world.

As a congregation of Christ's body in Goldsboro, North Carolina, we adopted the mission statement of Jesus from Luke's gospel: "The Spirit of the Lord is upon me, because he has anointed me to preach good news to the poor. He has sent me to proclaim release to the captives and recovering of sight to the blind, to set at liberty those who are oppressed, to proclaim the acceptable year of the Lord."[2]

Jesus's language was justice language—good news for the poor, freedom for prisoners, healing for the sick and oppressed. But it was clear that his ways were not the conventional political means. The freedom Jesus preached was rooted in the power of the "Spirit of the Lord" and made manifest in the "year of the Lord's favor." Liberation didn't come to first-century Palestine through the established political parties of the Pharisees or the Sadducees. Instead, Luke's gospel proclaimed that the freedom Jesus promised was already real in himself and, by the power of God's Spirit, in the acts of the apostles who followed Jesus. The church itself was called to be a liberation movement and a sign of what God's justice and freedom can mean for all people.

We started to look around in our neighborhood in Goldsboro and ask what good news might look like to our poor. After a few years, we established Rebuilding Broken Places, a community development corporation that could bring members of the church together with members of our local community to seek the peace of our city and build up justice for all. Because we saw how important education is to low-income children whose families have been generationally excluded from good work, we established an academy—a kind of freedom school, right there in the neighborhood, where kids could learn from people who looked like them that we expected them to succeed. We built forty units of senior housing and sixty single-family houses where low-income families could become first-time home owners, building equity for themselves and their children. We decided that Jesus's proclamation of "freedom to the captives" meant we needed to do something for young men coming home from prison. We set up a reentry program with classes designed to help those who carried the burden of a criminal history to find and keep good work.

Over the course of a decade, I watched our little congregation invest $1.5 million of its own money in the community. And I saw firsthand how that kind of coming together can inspire others to join you. Local businesses contributed. Friends across the state pitched in. We received some grants that were available for the kind of work we were doing and saw our church's investment increase tenfold. All of my life I'd felt a passion to see those living in bondage set free. Greenleaf showed me how that kind of liberation is the true work of the Spirit through the church. When we all get together, something powerful can happen.

From our education efforts to our housing work, Greenleaf was proud to say that our community engagement as a historically black church on behalf of the community impacted a diverse array of people. White, black, and Latino children were invited to study alongside one another, beginning in preschool, focusing on a curriculum built around attitude, academics, and the arts. From the beginning of our Community Development Corporation (CDC) work, we wrote it into the bylaws that the leadership of the church could never be employed by the CDC. We wanted to make sure it was always clear that this work was a way for the church to serve the community, not to make money off of it. As we studied the Scriptures together, this was simply what it meant for the church to be the church.

In my time at Duke Divinity School, I had read and heard the work of Stanley Hauerwas, who succeeded Reinhold Niebuhr as America's most well-known public theologian, though he was himself a harsh critic of Niebuhr. "The first task of the church is to be the church," Hauerwas argued, imagining a posture of social engagement which challenged Christian realism by saying that relevance and influence in the established social order was not the point; faithfulness to God's peculiar politics was what mattered. Only if the church is the church can people see that another way is possible. Without this alternative witness, we are tempted to think that the way things are is simply the way things have to be.

Greenleaf showed me the great value of Hauerwas's so-called "post-liberal" critique. It wasn't enough to see injustice and know that it is wrong. As my mentor Dr. William C. Turner said, "When the Spirit moves and we are saved . . . what follows is a challenge to the way things are."[3] In order for that challenge to be embodied as a social reality in this world, the Holy Spirit works to bring us together, making possible a way of life that none of us could pursue or even imagine on our own. This calling together—*ekklesia* in Greek—is what the New Testament calls "church." Greenleaf showed me what a New Testament church can look like in a small Southern town.

But our experience with Rebuilding Broken Places also made clear that the Spirit blows where it will, working in, through, and beyond the church. While it seemed that Professor Hauerwas and the postliberals were right about our need for the concrete example of a witness to God's justice in the world, it wasn't only the good church folk who made up that "city on a hill," shining the light of justice and love in our community. As a matter of fact, it was often folk outside the church who inspired us the most, standing as examples of what the church should be.

Holistic community development, rooted in the power of the Spirit, depended on its own kind of fusion coalition. Yes, we needed dedicated church folk with faith that not only motivated them but also gave them a distinct, prophetic vision for their work in the community. But we also needed community partners. We needed to come together with banks and businesspeople, with other people of faith and with people of no particular faith. When we went to share with others the vision we'd received from the Spirit, we found that the Spirit was often already moving them. The church didn't have a monopoly on God's dream. No, the Spirit was stirring all over the community.

As much as this pastoral experience taught me to appreciate Hauerwas's emphasis on the church's life together as its primary witness, it also challenged me to develop a more nuanced view of how the Spirit is at work in the world. I appreciated the longing for an alternative sociological reality where's God's justice and peace are experienced, yet I was disappointed by an imagination that could only anticipate that experience in the traditional spaces and practices of compromised Western

Christianity. Had not the liberating communities of the plantation South arisen in the brush arbors where there were no ordained clergy to celebrate the Eucharist or steeples to designate hallowed space? Were we not experiencing more gospel life in partnership with our Christian and non-Christian neighbors in the community than I had seen in many places called "church"?

Life as a Christian pastor compelled me to struggle intellectually toward a new imagination of faithful social engagement. Niebuhr's Christian realism, while it challenged me to think strategically, had been ultimately unsatisfying because it left too little space for the substance of things hoped for and the evidence of things not seen—for that greater moral vision which compels us to keep our eyes on the prize and hold on until freedom comes. On the other hand, Hauerwas's emphasis on the church's distinctive witness—a sort of "ecclesial realism"—helped me see the distinct gift of our life together at Greenleaf. But to the extent that it limited our vision of where the Spirit is at work in the world, this ecclesial realism mirrored Niebuhr's blind spot, obscuring our understanding of the liberating work God wants to do through the Spirit in all the world.

Intellectually, I was searching for a model of engagement that took seriously what I knew biblically, historically, and personally—namely, that fusion coalitions rooted in moral dissent have power to transform our world from the grassroots community up. In my study, I was watching and praying, thinking my way toward a new imagination. In the pulpit, I was preaching my way toward some new vision. But as in every movement, things were stirring beyond my control or foresight, preparing the way for a new statewide coalition to serve as a womb for the new form of social engagement that was only beginning to be conceived.

CHAPTER 4

From Banquets to Battle

A DOZEN YEARS as pastor at Greenleaf established the power of coalitions as my personal testimony. When the Spirit moved and brought us together as a community, we saw how God can change the world that is into the world that ought to be. This evidence of things hoped for buoyed the spirits of people who had long suffered without any genuine expectation for change. I watched how they walked with a new spring in their step, coming in and out of the Vision of Faith Community Center each day. Every preacher wants to hear their people shout when they preach the good news in a sermon. But it's a truly gratifying experience to see good news come to life in the neighborhood where you live and work. Like a doctor making rounds, I rode the streets within a two-mile radius of Greenleaf and watched a sick community becoming well.

One morning in early 2005, I got out of bed and went to the bathroom. For years I had always woken my wife up when I got up because I had to get my walker out and it would clank and bang. But as I was standing in the bathroom this particular morning, I realized I didn't have my walker. I thought I must be dreaming, so I went back to our bedroom and said to Rebecca, "Hey, wake up. Pinch me."

She opened her eyes and asked, "When did you get up?" For the first time in twelve years, I had walked to the bathroom and back without waking her up. We both laughed out loud. I knew we had become part of a community that was moving from sickness to health. But I had hardly noticed my own body getting well. It felt like one of those gospel stories where Jesus touched the lame and suddenly they could walk again. The day before, I'd been bent over that old walker. Now, I was moving around on my own two legs.

I went down the street that morning and bought a wooden cane. I've been carrying that same cane ever since. It's a raggedy old cane now, and people are always trying to give me new ones. But I say, "This cane is my testimony. The Lord said, 'Take up your mat and walk.'" So I carry it as a sign of what I learned from a community of people who came together in Goldsboro, North Carolina.

Words of the prophet Isaiah help me name the reality to which my old cane bears witness. Through the prophet, God asks Israel:

> Is not this the fast that I choose:
> to loose the bonds of wickedness,
> to undo the thongs of the yoke,
> to let the oppressed go free,
> and to break every yoke?
> Is it not to share your bread with the hungry,
> and bring the homeless poor into your house;
> when you see the naked, to cover him,
> and not to hide yourself from your own flesh?
> Then shall your light break forth like the dawn,
> and your healing shall spring up speedily.[1]

I've heard health and wealth preachers talk about the faith that's needed to be well in this world, but I decided after that morning in 2005 that Isaiah made clear what I must do for my own healing: I must help others to heal. Greenleaf's ministry had invited me into the up-close and personal work of unlocking handcuffs and untying yokes. It was the sort of work that made poverty personal because it gave justice issues a name and a face. We had, in fact, fed hungry people at our tables, listening to the stories of why they couldn't feed themselves. We had invited the homeless poor into homes, seeing firsthand how beloved children of God had been systemically excluded from the education, employment, and government services that folks on the other side of town enjoyed. Isaiah was right: they were our own flesh and blood. The poor looked like us and talked like us; when they were cut, they bled like us.

We had done some good work through Rebuilding Broken Places to set the oppressed free, but I had to be honest with myself. We had not, in the words of Isaiah, "broken every yoke." No matter how many people we helped in our little neighborhood in one Southern town, we knew things weren't going to change for them and for so many others in this world unless we challenged the power structure and changed the way our society works. Understanding my healing in the context of Isaiah's prophecy, I knew we had to do something more.

I remembered a commitment I had made years earlier, before my own hospitalization, when Rebecca and I traveled to Johns Hopkins for our young daughter to receive brain surgery. She had been diagnosed with serious hydrocephalus and we were doing everything in our power to reduce the swelling in her brain. As we were rushing in for the last appointment before her surgery, I noticed another little boy lying alone on a gurney in the hallway. Something inside me said, "So you're not concerned for this child, too?" I walked over and prayed for that boy before he went into surgery. Later that night, as Rebecca and I sat in the chapel, praying about our daughter's surgery, I felt like I had a small sense of what God must feel, watching a world where some of his children suffer and die from poverty and hunger while others play video games, knowing they will always have more than enough. I promised the Lord that night that I would dedicate my life to fighting for his vulnerable children.

Fifteen years later, my baby was a brilliant young woman, thriving because of good health care, a good education, and a family and community that loved her. But just as I had felt moved to pray for that other little boy at Johns Hopkins, I knew I had to stand up for God's children who weren't thriving because the yoke of oppression still weighed them down. If God had given me the strength to walk, then I was determined to hit the streets, spreading the good news of fusion coalitions to raise a cry of moral dissent and transform the systems of this world into a society of justice and peace.

Some friends of mine had encouraged me to run for state chapter president of the National Association for the Advancement of Colored People (NAACP). The oldest antiracist organization in America, the NAACP was founded as a fusion movement in 1909, when Dr. W. E. B. Du Bois, a highly educated African American, came together with white allies to say that the problem of the twentieth century was the problem of the color line. America could never achieve its promise of "liberty and justice for all" until it dealt with the legacy of slavery. Rooted in this racial analysis, the NAACP was and always had been a justice organization. Through the long days of Jim Crow, it built organizational power to challenge lynching and win the franchise for African Americans in the South. North Carolina's greatest organizer, Ms. Ella Baker, was a field secretary for the national NAACP office through the 1930s and '40s, establishing chapters throughout the South. In so many ways, there could have never been the fruit of a civil rights movement without the tilling and planting those NAACP chapters did at the grassroots level in Mississippi, Alabama, Georgia, South Carolina, and the Black Belt of North Carolina.

But I noted that, though it had this legacy of grassroots fusion coalition justice work, the NAACP in the twenty-first century had become a top-heavy social club for civil rights elites. Due to its long tenure, it was organizationally established, claiming more members than any other antiracist justice group in the country. But if the NAACP was to lead a twenty-first-century justice movement, it would have to reclaim its legacy and expand capacity through fusionist organizing.

In the summer of 2005, that same year I got off my walker and started to walk again, I ran for president of the North Carolina NAACP, campaigning to move us from "banquets to battle." We were not, I said, the National Association for Colored People. Our organization did not exist to hold fancy banquets where black folks could eat, drink, and be merry, remembering what the movement had done fifty years ago. No, the NAACP existed in 2005 to carry out the same work we'd been founded to do a century earlier—the work so many of our elders had sacrificed life and limb to carry forward. We were the National Association for the *Advancement* of Colored People. Our mission, I said, was to move forward, not backward.

The prophet Amos helped me name the situation we found ourselves in, both as an organization and as a nation at the beginning of the twenty-first century. A farmer in Israel in the eighth century before Christ, Amos was not a "court prophet." He wasn't an insider with the political elites of his day, but rather, in our modern language, a grassroots scholar and activist who had seen what bad social policy in Jerusalem could do to folks back home. When Amos spoke to his nation, his message was clear: "Woe unto you who are at ease in Zion." The great danger of achievement, Amos taught us, is that it leads to social amnesia.

In the course of my campaign, I made clear that black people did indeed have much to celebrate in 2005. We had survived the Middle Passage and endured 250 years of slavery to see that great Jubilee when, by the executive order of President Lincoln, all slaves were declared free. And though that freedom was curtailed and the promise of forty acres and a mule denied, we kept our eyes on the prize and defeated Jim Crow, dispelling the fear of lynch mobs and White Citizen Councils. When Jim Crow decided to go back to law school and become Mr. James Crow, Esquire, we fought him in the courts and in boardrooms, advocating for affirmative action and anti-discrimination policies. Yes, we could remember back in the day when we ate cucumber and tomato sandwiches because we couldn't afford any meat. But I told the members of the NAACP that we must, in the words of the young folk, keep it real. Most of us had more than enough for ourselves in 2005.

Our greatest temptation was to forget where we'd come from. Amos warned that, when we are at ease in Zion, we face two dangers. The first is to accommodate ourselves to an "acceptable" amount of injustice, conceding that things will, after all, never be perfect in this broken world. The second temptation is to not stand up against those forces that inevitably rise up to say, "We must go back to Egypt, where we lived as slaves."

I pointed out to the good people of the NAACP that although many of us were doing fine, the poor people we'd met in the neighborhood surrounding our church in Goldsboro had a different story to tell about the state of justice in America. Though some of us had crossed over to the American Dream, the gap between the median income of African Americans and the median income of whites had not changed at all since 1968. If a room full of black folks knew they were doing better than they had been doing fifty years before, then simple math made clear that, somewhere, there was another room full of black folks doing worse. I told them how the city schools in Goldsboro had essentially resegregated fifty-one years after *Brown v. Board of Education*. Although this was rooted in a history of racial injustice, I also pointed out that this injustice wasn't just about black people. Twelve percent of children in North Carolina had no health insurance.[2] That wasn't just black kids. Red and yellow, black and white, poor children were suffering from what Dr. King called the greatest injustice in the modern world—a lack of the basic care we all need to be well. Meanwhile, the single greatest institution shaping black life in America at the beginning of the twenty-first century was the prison industrial complex. More black men were in prison in 2005 than had been in slavery in 1850. Most of them would be coming home at some point, but the collateral consequences of their convictions meant that they could not go to college, find housing, gain employment, or vote.

Amos warned Israel in his day that when we are at ease in Zion, we too easily ignore the cries of hurting people, participating in what I've come to call "attention violence" by failing to respond to real people's real needs. But I told the delegates to the North Carolina NAACP convention that we who believe in freedom cannot rest. We know, as Amos knew, that our well-being is connected to the well-being of those who suffer. And we know that those who want to "take back America" don't have a point in history to take us back to where we experienced greater freedom. Even the strides forward that have been made cannot be preserved without vigilance. A justice movement can never circle camp and make celebrating past victories its primary function. No, the future of the NAACP must be as a militantly pro-justice, antiracist, antipoverty fusion coalition. If we were to have a future, I said, then it must be as a leader in helping America realize the promise of justice that had not yet been fulfilled.

Some were put off by this call to action. At the convention where the election was to be held, my wife sat down next to someone who was campaigning for one of the other candidates. He began to tell her about how I was trying to take over the NAACP and use the organization for personal gain. She listened politely, then smiled and said, "Well, if he were that bad, I can promise you I would have never married him."

Not everyone was immediately excited by a call to change, but Amos's message struck a chord with many and we won the election that summer. My task, then, was to pull together a team that could reflect this vision for what the NAACP should be. If we were going to go into battle as leaders of a new fusion coalition, we needed a leadership team to reflect our vision. We needed our veterans—black folks who'd sacrificed for generations to see the progress we could now enjoy. But we also needed faces that didn't look like us—young people and white folks who understood what it means to work with others as laborers for justice.

I asked Al McSurely, a white civil rights attorney who had worked with the Southern Conference Education Fund in the 1960s, to serve as legal redress chair for the NAACP. Al had fusion politics in his DNA. While organizing during the most intense years of the civil rights movement, he had seen his house blown up with dynamite in the North Carolina mountains and faced sedition charges in the state of Kentucky. Al defended himself all the way to the Supreme Court and became a constitutional lawyer in order to understand how our society's foundational laws protect the people's right to moral dissent. Al was a white

man, but he was just the sort of white man we needed to help lead the
NAACP into battle.

Although my first task as president was to travel the state, presenting
our vision to NAACP chapters and reengaging the membership, from
the beginning Al and I were talking about how we needed something
more—a coalition that extended beyond the base of the NAACP to
include others who were concerned about justice and the good of the
whole. The advancement of colored people had to be central because so
much of American injustice was rooted in our history of slavery. But the
NAACP's own history showed us that black folk can never move forward
by ourselves. We had to find a way to stand with others, acknowledging
their connections with us and our issues. Dr. King had understood this.
Civil rights could not be separated from worker's rights, so his Southern
Christian Leadership Conference had worked with many unions and
with the AFL-CIO. King's turn against the war in Vietnam and toward
the Poor People's Campaign in the last year of his life was an acknowl-
edgement of America's deep need to recognize how military spending
abroad was connected to lack of funding for the War on Poverty at
home. King was gunned down just as he was beginning to articulate our
need for a fusion coalition to work for the reconstruction of America.

I wrestled with these hard realities as I worked out a rhythm of traveling the state while my wife was at home during the week, then returning
to Goldsboro to be with the church and our kids on the weekend, when
Rebecca worked back-to-back shifts at the hospital. The state presidency
of the NAACP is a volunteer position, but I wasn't just volunteering my
own time. Our whole community was involved. For over twelve years,
I'd practiced doing nothing alone. Members of my church volunteered
to drive me everywhere I went for the NAACP. We'd visit twenty-five
people in a fellowship hall down east, then drive one hundred miles
to an NAACP chapter meeting at a Masonic Lodge in the Piedmont.
All the time I was looking for connections, showing up to support any
group in the state that was standing for justice. In a year of almost non-
stop travel, I learned something important about North Carolina: there

wasn't a huge crowd standing together in any one place, but if you added up all the different groups who were standing for their justice issue, the potential base for a coalition was large—bigger, I thought, than anything North Carolina had seen before.

Sometime during my travels in 2006, I started reading the prophet Ezekiel. Ezekiel was a dreamer who wrote about what he saw, speaking to the issues of his day even as he invited people to think about their shared future. In the last chapter of his book, Ezekiel concludes his prophecy with a grand vision of that great day when all of Israel's divided tribes would come together in Jerusalem. From east and west, north and south, he saw them streaming in to become a great congregation. And then, in the final verse, Ezekiel declared that when we all get together, the great city of Zion will itself be renamed. "And the name of the city henceforth shall be, The LORD is there."[3]

Thinking about the people I'd met across the state, I started to sketch a list of fourteen justice tribes in North Carolina. We had folks who cared about education, folks who cared about living wages, and others who were passionate about the 1.2 million North Carolinians who didn't have access to health care. We also had groups petitioning for redress for black and poor women who'd been forcibly sterilized in state institutions, organizations advocating for public financing in elections, and historically black colleges and universities petitioning for better state funding. I included on my list groups concerned about discrimination in hiring, others concerned about affordable housing, and people opposed to the death penalty and other glaring injustices in our criminal justice system. Finally, I noted the movements for environmental justice, immigrant justice, civil rights enforcement, and an end to America's so-called "war on terror." Any one of these "tribes" had several highly committed people who'd been working on their issue for years. Some of them had been able to mobilize thousands of people for a particular event, especially when their issue was a hot news item. But Ezekiel's bold vision got me thinking about what could happen if we all came together for a People's Assembly in our state capital, to show the members of the

General Assembly who their constituents are. What if the people most concerned about these fourteen different issues could form a twenty-first-century fusion coalition? Might such an assembly even give us new language and vision for the place where we gathered?

In December of 2006, we called a meeting of potential partners for this new coalition. Representatives of sixteen organizations showed up. We started with a blank sheet of butcher paper and asked each group to write the issue they were most concerned about. Then, on another sheet, we asked them to list the forces standing in the way of what their organization wanted. We learned something important at that first retreat: though our issues varied, we all recognized the same forces opposing us. What's more, we saw something that we hadn't had a space to talk about before: *There were more of us than there were of them.*

Just a couple of weeks later, I preached at a church in Raleigh. I talked about our recent retreat and read from Ezekiel's text, saying how his vision was inspiring a new movement in North Carolina. When I was finished, an older woman in that congregation stood up and said, "Did you hear how the Scripture ended? It says, 'The Lord is there.' It doesn't say he's going to be there. It says he's already there." She stood up in that church and told the people that the Lord was already on Jones Street, where the North Carolina General Assembly meets, and we needed to join God there.

Our new coalition partners decided to call a major teach-in and a march for citizens on the second Saturday in February 2007, declaring it North Carolina's first People's Assembly. Professor Jarvis Hall of North Carolina Central University led the committee, laying out a forum for citizenship education. We asked not only what the key issues were but also what our agenda should be. What action steps would be transformative for North Carolina? We came up with a fourteen-point agenda that outlined eighty-one action steps (complicated, for sure—but our coalition partners had been working on these issues for years). Then we chose a symbol for the movement that was based on our state constitution, because we knew our movement had to be deeply rooted in North

Carolina's most basic constitutional values and in our deepest moral values. We decided we would start the teach-in with "Did you know?" questions, making people aware of poor people's reality. Then we would outline the action steps under each agenda item, showing how we could achieve what we knew was good and right.

The night before that first People's Assembly, I spoke at a rally out in Henderson, about an hour's drive north of Raleigh. It was cold that night, and I was worried. People had warned us that we were crazy to try to rally people in the middle of the winter. Would folks really come out and march in the cold? I'll never forget showing up that next morning in Raleigh and seeing a few thousand people standing outside the Progress Energy Center (now the Duke Energy Center), where we were gathering for the teach-in. When we got inside the two-thousand-seat performance hall, it was a packed house, all the way to the back row of the balcony. After coalition partners presented each item, Stella Adams stood up and called for a vote, and the fourteen-point agenda was adopted unanimously. Then we marched through downtown Raleigh to Jones Street and stood in front of the State Legislative Building to publicly present our agenda. Like Martin Luther nailing his ninety-five theses to the door of the church in Wittenberg at the beginning of the Reformation, we posted our fourteen points outside the State Legislative Building on a fourteen-foot-high placard. Black and white, young and old, the coalition we had only imagined fifty days earlier was standing before us on the Fayetteville Mall. It was an astounding sight.

Al McSurely had come up with a name: Historic Thousands on Jones Street (HKonJ). He said our movement was historic because such a diverse coalition had never gathered to stand together before a statehouse. It was focused on Jones Street because we knew we couldn't change America without changing states. And we were thousands because people needed to see with their own eyes the diversifying electorate of our state and of America. Publicizing HKonJ had been more or less an act faith for us—not knowing who all would show up. But here we were—it *was* Historic Thousands on Jones Street. It was almost as if the people were out in front of us, showing us something we could hardly find language to describe. I'll never forget the scene of all those people coming forward to sign their names to the fourteen-point agenda. A woman came to me with tears in her eyes and said, "I want to thank you for calling us together. I didn't know. I just didn't know."

Indeed, we had not known the extent of others' pain and suffering until we came together to listen. We did not know how much we had in common until we told our stories of struggle to one another. What's more, we didn't know our own power until we gathered as one coalition with a moral agenda. We could not have known as we stood on the Fayetteville Mall that cold Saturday morning what our movement would become. But six and a half years later, after Moral Mondays had become a national news story, reporters asked me to explain how thousands of people had spontaneously decided to protest, risking arrest and escalating our resistance every week for thirteen weeks. Where had this movement come from?

I didn't pretend I could explain *how* a movement had been born. But when people asked where it came from, I told them about that first HKonJ. We had first gathered on Jones Street when Democrats were in power. We had said from the beginning that our agenda wasn't Republican or Democrat, liberal or conservative. We weren't advocating for left or right, but for all that is good *and* right. We had studied our history. We knew that fusion politics were central to our state's history. In 1868, before the Fusion Party won seats in an election, a black preacher named J. W. Hood and a white preacher named Samuel Stanford Ashley had worked together to rewrite our state constitution. Echoing Jefferson's Declaration of Independence, they wrote that all people are "endowed by their Creator with certain unalienable Rights." But in view of North Carolina's history of race-based slavery, they made a significant addition to Mr. Jefferson's list. "Among them," they insisted, "are life, liberty, *the enjoyment of the fruits of their own labor*, and the pursuit of happiness" (emphasis mine). When men whose labor had been stolen through chattel slavery had a say in writing a new constitution, they declared that a just compensation for labor is an inalienable right. They went on to say that "beneficent provision for the poor, the unfortunate . . . is among the first duties" of our state. And they affirmed, as a matter of democratic principle, that all power of our state's government is derived from the people.[4]

These lofty notions were not proposals for the future of North Carolina. They were constitutional guarantees that had been on the books for nearly 150 years. It didn't matter what the polls said or what campaign promises a politician made. Anyone who took the oath of office swore to uphold this constitution. From the very beginning, the HKonJ People's Assembly insisted that we were going to hold our elected officials to their oath and stand for North Carolina's deepest constitutional values.

Because our agenda was comprehensive, covering fourteen issue areas where we could move forward together with specific action steps, many asked us in the weeks following our assembly on Jones Street, "Which issues are your priority for this session? What do you want to achieve first?"

We explained that, for us, every issue was equally important. In a fusion coalition, our most directly affected members would always speak to the issue closest to their own hearts. But they would never speak alone. When workers spoke up for the right to organize and engage in collective bargaining, the civil rights community would be there with them. And when civil rights leaders petitioned for the expansion of voting rights for people of color, white workers would stand with them. Again, we knew our history. The power of the abolitionist movement through the nineteenth century, the fusionist movement in the post-Reconstruction era, and the civil rights movement in the mid-twentieth century was always the same: a diverse coalition of people with shared moral concern, refusing to be divided by fear or intimidation. In the 1960s, the white power structure of the South had resisted fusionist power in direct ways, allowing the terrorism of the Klan and employing explicit language of hate and fear. When George Wallace lost the Alabama gubernatorial race to John Patterson in 1958, he famously promised to "never be out-niggered again." Wallace became an icon of overt racism, declaring after being elected governor four years later, "Segregation now, segregation tomorrow, segregation forever!"

But by the late 1960s, mainstream America had sided with the civil rights movement on the issue of desegregation, making clear its distaste for the language of hatred and fear. Those who wanted to maintain power shifted gears, adopting for the Republican Party what Richard Nixon's advisor Kevin Phillips dubbed "the Southern Strategy." The goal, as always, was to divide and conquer. But the language was not as overt as the segregationists'. Rather than talking about segregation and "our Southern way of life," politicians called for "law and order." They began to attack "entitlement programs," playing on the fears of poor whites who had themselves benefited from Social Security and the GI Bill. As long as the movement's coalition could be divided by other means, racist language wasn't needed. The Southern Strategy protected white power while appearing to be color-blind.

But after forty years of wandering in the wilderness, isolated in our issue-based tribes, our HKonJ coalition found others to stand with them on Jones Street. Like a cloud by day and a fire by night, our common agenda, rooted in North Carolina's deepest moral and constitutional values, promised to lead us forward. We did not know how long we would have to struggle or how many obstacles we would have to overcome. But we made three commitments to one another after that first HKonJ: (1) we would stay together until we saw our People's Agenda become the agenda of North Carolina's government; (2) we would go home and gather People's Assemblies in our cities and towns, building up this fusion coalition; and (3) we would come back next year on the second Saturday in February.

We had held up our vision and sent out a battle cry; now we had an army. But our troops were more like the ad hoc militias of the American Revolution than the well-trained battalions of modern militaries. A boot camp would have benefited most of us, but in the event, our lessons in nonviolent struggle would come on the field of battle.

CHAPTER 5

Resistance Is
Your Confirmation

ALMOST NO ONE outside North Carolina noticed our first HKonJ. But that was not a negative. In movement building, this is an important point to remember. Though we knew we were witnessing something historic—though our deepest moral convictions told us this was right— we had very little external affirmation, even after a mobilization that showed us what a new moral movement looked like. They say "seeing is believing," but the truth is that those in power will ignore what they do not want to see as long as we let them. We who believe in freedom and justice must remember the summary of nonviolent struggle often attributed to Gandhi: "First they ignore you. Then they laugh at you. Then they fight you. Then you win."

While they are ignoring you, you have time to build power.

This is what our twenty-first-century fusion coalition did in 2007. Our agenda was comprehensive, covering the full scope of our partner's issues, yet we knew from fusion history that we could not advance the people's agenda unless we built power by expanding voting rights. In 1866, when North Carolina's first fusion movement was just beginning, the Reverend J. W. Hood, a pastor in the African Methodist Episcopal Zion Church, stood before the North Carolina Constitutional Convention and said, "Let us have faith, and patience, and moderation, yet assert always that we want three things,—first, the right to give evidence in the courts; second, the right to be represented in the jury-box; and third, the right to put votes in the ballot box. These rights we want, these rights we contend for, and these rights, under God, we must ultimately have."[1]

Hood was right, both morally and historically. Without power in the courts and in the legislature, a pro-justice fusion coalition could never defeat white supremacy. But if voting rights were expanded to include African Americans, then they could join their forces with other antiracist, pro-justice coalitions in America. The expansion of voting rights was a bedrock of fusion politics from the very beginning.

More blacks were elected to public office during the period from 1868 to 1880 than at any other time in American history. During this first fusion movement, blacks and whites joined together to reconstruct the nation in ways that would make it possible to move toward the noble goals of justice and equality. Some of the most progressive economic, educational, and labor laws in our nation's history were passed during this era.

Almost a century before the Voting Rights Act of 1965, sixteen African Americans were elected to seats in the US Congress; more than six hundred black men took the oath of office in Southern state legislatures between 1865 and 1880. Although they never held office in proportion to their numbers, African Americans wielded significant power in every statehouse. In North Carolina more African Americans served in the state legislature than are there today. Though Southern white terrorism and Northern white indifference destroyed Reconstruction, the redefinition of American citizenship is unimaginable without the framework of rights won by these black and white pioneers of fusion politics. They attacked the divisive rhetoric of white solidarity and pointed to the common interests of most black and white Southerners.

During Reconstruction, these fusion coalitions took power. In the decade following America's Civil War, more than a quarter of white voters in the South cast their ballots for black-majority coalitions. In the 1890s, a Fusion Party made up of Republicans and Populists in North Carolina swept the state legislature, and won both the two US Senate seats and the governorship. These fusion coalitions of blacks and whites in the South passed some of the most progressive educational and labor laws in our nation's history, guaranteeing publicly funded education not only for all children, but for "all persons." (Former slaves had been denied access to education and even basic literacy for generations.) Those whose labor had been stolen codified the "just fruit of their own labor" as a God-given right of all people. They did all of this by bringing people together around a deeply moral, antiracist, pro-justice people's agenda. But they did not stop there. As the Reverend Hood saw so clearly here in North Carolina, the accomplishments of fusion coalitions depend upon the expansion of voting rights—rights that "under God, we must ultimately have."

In our public memory of the civil rights movement, to be understood as a Second Reconstruction, we often forget that this same insight about the fundamental need for voting rights was at the heart of the movement from the beginning. Sloppy and romantic renderings of our struggle suggest that Rosa Parks sat down on that bus because she was tired and Martin Luther King stood up to defend her. Inspired by their witness of direct action, we say, students integrated lunch counters and buses in the early sixties. Only then, in this telling, did the white liberal establishment deign to grant black people civil rights in 1964 and voting rights in 1965.

Fact is, the civil rights movement of the sixties itself was the result of fusion coalitions that saw the fundamental need to expand voting rights from the very beginning. Rosa Parks didn't sit down because she was tired. She sat down in an intentional, strategic act of civil disobedience because she had attended a workshop at the Highlander Folk School, in Monteagle, Tennessee, where local community leaders spent two weeks together planning strategies for integration. In that context of fusion organizing—black and white together—she said she woke up for the first time in her life to the smell of bacon that a *white person was cooking for her*. Coming together in that way gave her the vision and nonviolence gave her and Dr. King the tools to demonstrate their capacity for struggle.

But Dr. King was clear from 1957—the year after they desegregated Montgomery's buses—that the single most important goal for an antiracist, pro-justice, fusion coalition in America was the expansion of voting rights. At the Prayer Pilgrimage for Freedom, the March on Washington that preceded the one we remember by six and a half years, King concluded the day with a speech entitled "Give Us the Ballot." When Eisenhower was president and Lyndon Johnson was still leading the Democrats in the Senate, Dr. King said, "Our most urgent request to the president of the United States and every member of Congress is to give us the right to vote." With the ballot, King foresaw, black people would have political power that they could use to partner with others in coalitions to challenge the powers of injustice.

Though King's articulation of an agenda that pushed beyond reform to reconstruction would not be fully developed for nearly a decade, he saw from the beginning of his fusion building efforts what the Reverend Hood had attested to almost a century before him: America cannot move forward from our history of racial division without the expansion of voting rights.

When our HKonJ coalition came together in 2007, Dr. Timothy Tyson, professor of history at Duke University, often reminded us how the established powers had conspired to give "black power" a bad name. But black power joined with the economic and electoral power of fusion partners, Dr. Tyson said, was the only thing that had ever moved this country forward. If we wanted to move forward together with our People's Agenda, history taught us that we had to expand voting rights.

The Supreme Court of the United States, as it happened, had confirmed on record what William Faulkner expressed so succinctly in *Requiem for a Nun*: "The past is never dead. It's not even past." Writing for the Court in its 1986 decision in *Thornburg v. Gingles*, Justice William Brennan noted that "North Carolina had officially discriminated against its black citizens with respect to their exercise of the voting franchise from approximately 1900 to 1970 by employing at different times a poll tax, a literacy test, a prohibition against bullet (single-shot) voting, and designated seat plans for multimember districts."[2] In the twentieth century we had documented cases of intentional voter suppression for the first seven decades. Though those barriers had been removed, their effects continued. Justice Brennan went on to say that black voter registrations remained low—just over 50 percent of those eligible to vote in 1982.

After generations of officially prohibiting blacks from voting, the white power structure of North Carolina had found quieter, more subtle ways to suppress the electoral power of black and poor people. Once again, Jim Crow had cleaned up his language, put on a suit, and continued to rule as James Crow, Esquire. But we knew we had history on our side. We knew we had the Voting Rights Act and legal precedents such as the *Thornburg* decision on our side. We knew we had on our side the God who brought down Goliath with David's single stone. So we set out in 2007 to expand voting rights.

By the end of the legislative session, we had a crucial win. Both houses approved a bill that both expanded early voting and made same-day registration possible. In our research, we had learned that the primary reason poor people did not vote was because they didn't have a day off from work on Election Day. Though North Carolina's constitution guaranteed free elections, folks struggling to make ends meet on hourly pay simply could not afford to miss a day—or even an hour—and risk losing their fragile employment. They certainly didn't have time to travel to their county board of elections months prior to November, make sure their paperwork was in order, and then get off work again on a weekday to vote at their local precinct. Due to the highly mobile nature of low-wage work, many working poor people told us that they were often hours away from their precinct on Election Day, building someone else's home or cleaning a school miles away from their own children.

Expanding voting rights in the twenty-first century, we learned, meant overcoming middle-class assumptions about when and where "free" elections can happen. If a poor person could show up anywhere she happened to be working on Election Day and both register and vote on that same day, more poor people would be free to vote. What's more, if poor people could register and vote on the weekend prior to Election Day, voting rights would be further expanded, allowing folks to spend a precious day off voting for candidates who represent their interests in local, state, and federal government. Politicians weren't addressing poor people's concerns because they knew in a very real sense that they were not going to have to answer to poor people on Election Day. The legislation we helped to push through in 2007 challenged that assumption. It opened the door for the first significant expansion of voting rights in North Carolina in half a century.

But movement work doesn't just happen in a statehouse. Once we had the governor's signature on this important piece of legislation, we had to turn our attention to educating and mobilizing people to get out and vote. Coalition partners proved invaluable in this work. We got the word out through our established networks, launching a grassroots education effort that "went viral," as they say, because of the reach of multiple overlapping organizations that represented millions of North Carolinians. Through the NAACP, we launched a "Souls to the Polls" campaign, organizing black churches to provide free transportation to early-voting sites after worship services. Some ministers expressed concern because they had been misinformed. They thought their churches might risk their nonprofit status if they engaged in "political activity"— they had been sent misleading information. But we provided them with documentation to show that nonpartisan support of their members' constitutional right to vote was not only legal—it was a moral mandate, deeply rooted in our faith traditions. Democracy as a form of government might only be a few centuries old. But the value of every child of God for the good of the whole is a principle as old as the Torah.

In keeping with the Gandhian formula, most political pundits and party strategists in the country simply ignored us. Occasionally we would see mean-spirited cartoons, most of them poking fun at me personally. If we had been in this for external rewards, it would have been an exercise in daily frustration. The pay was nonexistent, the accolades absent, the mockery mean, and the encouragements few and far between. But we knew that what we were doing was right. And we had each other. Nothing could have been more rewarding than traveling my own home state, week after week, speaking into dark and desperate situations and watching people come to life. Ezekiel had given me the initial inspiration for HKonJ. As our coalition built real political power from the ground up through 2007 and 2008, I felt like I was witnessing Ezekiel's valley of dry bones, where the Spirit blew and broken pieces started joining back together again. I'd grown up singing the spiritual about "dem bones, dem bones, dem dry bones." Now I felt like I was watching them resurrected in real time.

The presidential election of 2008 raised the curtain on our coalition's appearance on the public stage. Because we were a coalition and not a single organization, the analysts and commentators didn't know at first how to make sense of what they saw. They only knew that something had happened in North Carolina that no one had expected—something that hadn't been seen since Ronald Reagan's New Beginning in 1980. All fifteen of North Carolina's Electoral College votes went to a Democrat. What's more, he was a black man. The margin was slim—about a third of a percent, or just over 100,000 votes. But when they ran the numbers on new voters, it became clear that the expansion of voting rights in 2007 had added at least 185,000 new voters to the 2008 electorate, most of whom had voted for change. The people had spoken clearly in the only language that those in power could hear. Almost overnight, we moved to a new stage of battle. Our days of quiet organizing and capacity building were over. We were under attack.

At our NAACP office, death threats started coming in. Mean-spirited ideologues were no longer content to poke fun at me as "Reverend Bar-B-Q." They felt threatened by our coalition's power and fell back on the fears that had been passed down to them by their parents and grandparents. If a black man was president, America must be out of control. We were accused of being part of a Marxist conspiracy and told that, in various parts of the state, they knew how to deal with men like me and President Obama. Pictures of nooses came across our fax machine with some regularity. They were a vivid image of the fear that our power inspired.

This was the twenty-first century, of course, but this response felt familiar. Fusion politics was as threatening to the white power structure in 2008 as it had been in 1868—the year the KKK was founded, the same year when J. W. Hood and Samuel Stanford Ashley had worked so hard to write a new vision for North Carolina into our constitution. In response to nineteenth-century fusion organizing, the Klan murdered the first black town councilman in Graham, North Carolina, hanging his body in the town square. They killed a white Republican in Caswell County. Terrorism alone has never been the primary means of maintaining power within American democracy, but the threat of it has often sufficed to sustain a politics of fear within the masses. When North Carolina's Fusion Party government was overthrown in 1898, gun-wielding Red Shirts—white-supremacist paramilitaries—drove elected officials out of office and burned down most of black-owned Wilmington, North Carolina. The Democratic Party stood in as the official authority to take back control for the moneyed elites.

Although many things had changed in the intervening century, the dynamics of power remained very much the same. We knew that the most dangerous extremists were not sitting in their home offices, sending nasty faxes (though we had to take those threats seriously). The people most frightened by our fusion coalition were the elites who had inherited the spoils of white power and had run North Carolina by proxy for generations. Thus, our most powerful enemies were neither the fear-driven terrorists nor their puppet kings, but the quiet kingmakers. They were flying to private meetings with their peers in other states, developing a strategy to fight back against a movement they had falsely hoped they could ignore. What they had on their side, they knew, was money. As shrewd businessmen, they plotted to invest it well on two fronts: a legal battle in the courts and a grassroots struggle for control of the statehouse.

Their most important legal battle turned out to be the case *Citizens*

United v. The Federal Election Commission.[3] Although purporting to be a case about free speech, the fundamental issue—the one that mattered most to wealthy power brokers threatened by poor people's votes—was whether corporations would be allowed unlimited investment in political campaigns. Winning by a 5–4 decision, Citizens United and others determined to "take back America" were given free rein to pour mystery money into the 2010 midterm elections. The timing couldn't have been better for extremists in North Carolina, for they had already decided that the battle to be won was right here at home, in our state legislature races.

At the center of this effort to subvert our fusion coalition's power was Art Pope, the ultraconservative head of a regional five-and-dime retail chain. A younger Pope had learned state politics as a legislator and pro bono counsel to various conservative campaigns. But after inheriting his father's business, Pope came to see that his real power was in strategic investment of his family's considerable financial resources. A protégé of the men who had developed the Southern Strategy a generation earlier, Pope was skilled in the mechanics of defending institutionalized racism without using the language of race. A gentle, religious man, he spoke quietly about small government, fiscal responsibility, and the inefficiencies of government programs. To a public that hardly knew him, he was an honest businessman willing to offer his financial skills in public service. But off the record, in secret meetings with power brokers across the state, Pope was plotting a takeover of North Carolina's government.

Through an array of foundations and organizations set up to influence public opinion, Art Pope contributed about a tenth of the $30 million invested in local campaigns for seats in the state House of Representatives across North Carolina in 2010. His investment paid off: extremists determined to "take back" control of the legislature won a majority of seats by using the politics of fear to rally Republican voters. Of course, none of these campaigns was overtly racist. No one used the N-word (not in public, at least). But after this new Republican majority had elected its speaker, Representative Thom Tillis, someone posted a video of him on YouTube in which he is seen explaining to a room of white people how "we have to find a way to divide and conquer the people who are on assistance."[4] He went on to explain how he wanted a woman with cerebral palsy who "deserves" government assistance to "look down on those people" who, unlike her, choose to be in the condition they're in and therefore deserve nothing. It was a textbook example of racism without overt racists. Kevin Phillips, creator of the Southern Strategy, would have been proud.

But we had to face facts: this man was the officially recognized leader of our legislature, backed by an extremist majority. Though our HKonJ fusion coalition had demonstrated incredible power, coming together across old dividing lines and expanding voting rights, we had also suffered a serious blow. With less than $20,000 of our organization's own money (and lots of volunteer hours), we'd built some basic organizational infrastructure for issue-based organizations to join hands and work together. In response, extremists had invested tens of millions of dollars—much of the money from outside North Carolina—in a campaign to discredit our efforts, demonize the poor, and stir up old fears that have divided the South for decades. In real and measurable ways, we were losing ground.

But as sobering as the political realists' assessment was, we knew we were in a profoundly moral struggle. Extremists had not focused their energies and investments on North Carolina because we were weak. They were throwing all they had at us because we were strong. No, we didn't have money on our side. And because we lacked money, we didn't have the organizational capacity, the access to the influential, or the ear of the media that they did. What we had on our side was truth. We had love and justice and the faith that, if we could just hold on for a little while longer, goodness would win out in the end. Maybe the Pope machine was a Goliath. Still, with a few smooth stones and God on our side, we knew we could stand our ground.

Because I'd spent my whole adult life preaching the message of Jesus, I also knew something he showed us at the very beginning of his public ministry: that resistance is our confirmation. In Luke's gospel, when Jesus steps onto the public stage in his hometown of Nazareth, he chooses

[Handwritten note at top:] Fan Mail Address Barack Obama Office of Barack and Michelle Obama

[Handwritten note right margin:] P.O. Box 9100 Washington, D.C. 20066 USA 202-464-6963 USA 60615 USA

for his first sermon the text that had become so central to our work at Greenleaf Christian Church, the passage from the prophet Isaiah that begins, "The Spirit of the LORD is upon me, because he has anointed me to preach good news to the poor." Calling the oppressed and divided people of the Galilee together, Jesus electrified the crowd with this message of liberation and hope. People came to life when they saw, through Jesus's ministry, that a world of justice and peace is possible. But that is not the end of the story in Luke, chapter 4. Luke is painfully honest in his telling. He concludes the story of Jesus's first sermon by saying, "And they rose up and put him out of the city, and led him to the brow of the hill on which their city was built, that they might throw him down headlong. But passing through the midst of them he went away."[5]

This is, of course, a central theme of the gospel story which ends not with Jesus taking Jerusalem through a popular uprising but with Jesus being executed as an enemy of the state. Yet, two thousand years later, the history of Israel and Rome are measured in time marked before and after the One they crucified. Faith-rooted moral battles are not won with the world's weapons and they do not always advance on schedules that make sense to us. But of this we can always be sure: when we stand for what is good and right, evil will employ every power at its disposal to take us out. A heavy backlash against our movement for justice may hurt. It may well make us weep and moan. But it must not deter us. In fact, it should encourage us. Because resistance is our confirmation that we are on the right track.

Frederick Douglass taught us back in the nineteenth century that power concedes nothing without a demand. Because power blinds broken human beings to injustice, the most powerful among us will always ignore and laugh at the cries of those who suffer. But when the balance of power tips far enough to threaten those who think they are in control—when the people come together in a demonstration of our political force—*then* those in power fight back. Their resistance is our confirmation that we are gaining ground. When they stop laughing and start fighting, you can be sure they are worried that you are winning.

[Handwritten note at bottom:] Address Information Barack Obama Foundation 5235 S. Harper Court Suite 1140 Chicago, IL

If we had accepted the liberal consensus that suggests that faith is either divisive or inherently regressive, we would have never had the resources to stand our ground after the initial backlash of 2008. But those years of struggle solidified in our coalition the need for a faith-rooted, moral movement that welcomes people of all faiths, as well as those who struggle with faith. A diverse coalition of liberals and conservatives, Christians, Jews, and Muslims, the documented and the undocumented, black, white, and brown sisters and brothers were learning that we could trust one another. What's more, we could trust a Higher Power to have our back when things got rough. This faith even gave us hope to pray that our enemies might become our friends.

While we held on to faith and stood our ground, there was work to be done. Resistance did more than confirm our purpose; it challenged us to go deeper with one another and with our analysis of the situation at hand. As with every partnership, we had to move past the honeymoon and deal with the real stuff we each brought to the table. The "enemy," as it turned out, wasn't always out there. Sometimes, the enemy was us. To move forward together, we would have to deal with unquestioned assumptions and internalized fears. Thankfully, the opposition gave us plenty of reason to keep coming together.

CHAPTER 6

Many a Conflict,
Many a Doubt

WHEN JESUS SAID, "Love your enemies," he wasn't simply stating a spiritual ideal to strive toward; he was also offering strategic advice for long-term success in any freedom struggle. Gandhi took this advice seriously and developed it into a philosophy of nonviolence, which came to America through the Montgomery bus boycott of 1955–56. After a year of battle, which concluded with a Supreme Court decision ordering the integration of Montgomery's buses, Martin Luther King Jr. made clear that the nonviolent struggle was not over. As St. Paul says in the book of Romans, we are *more than conquerors* when we engage in a moral struggle. It's not enough to conquer the opposition. In a nonviolent struggle, we are committed to fight on until we win our adversaries as friends. As King explained to his Montgomery congregation, "The significant thing is that when you follow this way, when the battle is almost over, a new friendship and reconciliation exists between the people who have been the oppressors and the oppressed."[1]

This is the end goal of nonviolent struggle: a new nation—a new world—where former enemies become co-laborers for the common good. We can never be friends with our enemies, of course, until they stop trying to destroy us. But even in the midst of a struggle, Jesus said, we can love our enemies. As love seeks understanding, we can learn from them. Sometimes, in fact, they become our most important teachers as we develop tactics for the next stage of battle.

Because our coalition had inherited this philosophy of nonviolent struggle from the Southern freedom movement, we did not stop at seeing the resistance of extremist forces as a confirmation of our moral cause. We also considered their massive attack against us as an opportunity to learn.

How had it been possible for these extremists to stir up old fears and convince poor white people to vote against their own interests? Money, of course, was part of the answer. But money has to be invested in something. As I thought about our movement, I paid attention to the infrastructure that Art Pope and others had worked so long and hard to build. When we followed the money, we found that the great majority of it had not been invested in political campaigns. Most had gone to foundations and media corporations that were invested in shaping culture. The products of this machine weren't candidates as much as interns and fellows at foundations, as well as op-eds, ad campaigns, press releases, media packets, and educational materials. By telling North Carolina a story about where we had come from and where we were going, the Southern Strategy introduced cultural memes every bit as powerful as the Confederate flag or a lynch mob's noose. Only now, their buzzwords were "entitlements," "big government," and "the undeserving poor." They didn't need to tell people who to vote for. Any candidate could play to their base by using words they'd taught people to hate.

Our opposition helped me to see clearly that our fusion coalition's work wasn't primarily political but cultural. If we were to overcome the divide-and-conquer strategy being used against us, we had to learn how to offer North Carolina powerful images of solidarity—not just at our annual People's Assembly but in daily acts of justice and community building. Those determined to "take back America" helped us see how the battle, while deeply political, wasn't fundamentally about campaigns and elections. Long before people went to the polls, our struggle was to reshape the stories that tell us who we are.

Too often those stories were about one group's interests versus another's. We learned that workers at the Smithfield hog-processing plant in Tar Heel, North Carolina, had been trying to organize a union for over a decade. They had been intimidated, attacked, and harassed by the factory bosses of this five-thousand-worker facility. And they had made little headway. In the media as well as in the community, the story was simply one of worker's interests versus business interest. The workers were saying they couldn't survive on the wages they were getting. Smithfield replied that they couldn't afford to pay more. Most folks who heard anything about it simply couldn't see how this fight had anything to do with the rest of us.

The Reverend Nelson Johnson, who had been helping the workers, helped us to see that this was a perfect case for us to change the narrative by making the workers' struggle a moral cause for our whole coalition. First, we went to Tar Heel and listened to the people who worked in the factory. We visited their humble homes and met those whose bodies had been broken by the work of slaughtering thousands of hogs each night. We looked into their eyes and heard them say, "We don't have enough to pay the rent and feed our families." These workers were not an "issue." They were beloved children of God, crying out for help.

In a fusion coalition, we knew the Smithfield workers had to tell their own story. They were the moral witnesses to the injustice they had experienced. But they could not stand alone. The exploitation of their labor was deeply rooted in North Carolina's history of slavery, sharecropping, and union busting. These workers were predominantly people of color, but the Smithfield bosses were trying to use cultural differences between black and brown—immigrants from Latin America—to drive a wedge between them. Our HKonJ coalition came alongside them to say, "We're in this together. We can't be divided. Let's stand strong and stand together."

At grocery stores across the state, we coordinated local clergy and community leaders to make a public statement asking that they stop carrying Smithfield meats until the factory recognized the union and negotiated a contract with the company. In local news outlets throughout the state, people saw women and men they knew and respected standing with workers they had never met. It changed the narrative. The public story was no longer one about workers versus bosses. It was about the moral challenge of people receiving the just fruit of their labor, a principle enshrined in our state constitution. Though the company held out for months, trying on multiple occasions to scare us away or buy us off, we stood our ground together. Eventually, the union was recognized, a good contract was negotiated, and the relationship between our coalition and labor unions deepened. Whenever we called on people to mobilize, those Smithfield workers would show up in their bright-yellow T-shirts. Black and brown, they would march together.

In a 1965 speech to the Illinois State AFL-CIO, Dr. King had outlined the need for civil rights and labor activists to join forces. "The two most dynamic Movements that reshaped the Nation the past three decades are the labor and civil rights Movements," he said. "If our two Movements unite their social pioneering initiative, thirty years from now people will look back on this day and honor those who had the vision to see the full possibilities of modern society and the courage to fight for their realization."[2] It had taken us over forty years, but we were beginning to catch up to Dr. King's vision. We learned from experience that he was right: at the heart of a moral movement for a just economy we had to bring workers together with freedom fighters who had a deeply antiracist analysis of our nation's economic problems. Conversations about "fair wages" or "civil rights" could not be reduced to the self-interest of separate groups. No, we were engaged together in a conversation about what kind of economy builds up the common good.

The onset of the Great Recession at the end of 2008 only created more space for us to push this fundamental reconsideration of economic priorities. When so many folks' 401k's turned into 101k's, they saw what poor people have always known: that an economy built on the backs of slave labor simply doesn't work for most citizens. People who had worked themselves blue in the face arguing against "government intervention" prevailed upon the government to bail out the biggest banks because these banks, we were told, were "too big to fail." After 250 years of forced labor, freed slaves had not even gotten forty acres and mule, but these so-called conservatives were suggesting that banks that had overspeculated deserved our tax money to shore up their books and keep things going so they could eventually lend our money back to us at interest. As poor people came together across old racial dividing lines, we were able to make clear how little sense this made for any of us.

We began to identify pro-labor, antipoverty policies that ensure economic sustainability as a centerpiece of our agenda. A fusion coalition committed to the common good could bring black, white, and brown together, insisting on an economy that works for everyone. But to stand together, we would have to listen to one another and understand the other pressures that weighed heavily on some of our partners as they struggled to survive in this society.

John McNeil, a native of Wilson, North Carolina, became a teacher to many of us on one of the most fundamental injustices in our society: racial inequity in our criminal justice system. Back in 2005, John, who was a middle-aged business owner, had been confronted at his home in Georgia by a white man wielding a box cutter. After John asked the man to leave several times, the situation escalated as John's assailant threatened John's son. Fearing for his family, John shot at the trespasser, later identified as Brian Epp. Epp was killed by the bullet from John's gun. Police investigators were called to the scene immediately, conducted an investigation, and reported the killing as a case of self-defense.

But almost a year later, local prosecutors decided to bring first-degree murder charges against John, a black man, for killing a white man. John was tried, found guilty, and sentenced to life in prison. This is when we learned about the case from the local NAACP branch in Wilson.

For the NAACP, this was an all-too-familiar story. Since our struggle against lynching in the early twentieth century, the NAACP has been painfully aware of the way Southern justice is plagued by racial disparity in enforcement, prosecution, and sentencing. Now, John's case gave us the opportunity to address this injustice as a fusion coalition. What if it wasn't just black people standing up for John? What if black, white, and brown could stand together to say injustice anywhere is a threat to justice everywhere. We decided to take on John's case not simply as the NAACP, but as the HKonJ coalition.

About that time, Bob Zellner, a veteran of the 1960s Student Non-violent Coordinating Committee (SNCC), was passing through North Carolina en route to a speaking engagement in Charleston. He stopped in to visit some old friends and learned about John's case. Bob had re-cently decided to move to New Orleans, where he'd organized workers in the 1970s, to help with relief efforts following Hurricane Katrina. But the movement here in North Carolina intercepted him. Bob decided to move to Wilson and support the campaign for John McNeil's freedom.

A native of lower Alabama, Bob fit right in among white folks in a small Southern town. His grandfather had been a Klansman, his father a Bible-toting evangelist who'd named him Bob after the conservative white evangelist Bob Jones. He was, in short, not the sort of septuage-narian Southerner most people expected to stand up for a black man. But Bob had fusion politics in his veins from his SNCC days. He had been welcomed into the movement by Dr. King and Rosa Parks, then trained in organizing by Ella Baker through SNCC. Bob told stories of getting Klansmen and black woodcutters in Louisiana to organize unions in the seventies. His leadership was just what we needed to help our young fusion coalition see how racial disparity in our criminal jus-tice system was a moral issue for all of us.

Whereas the Smithfield struggle had played out in boardroom ne-gotiations, the fight to free John was a legal battle. We leaned heavily on the good lawyers that the NAACP brought to the table. But we also recognized that we were trying this case in the court of public opinion. In America's legal system, prosecutors are elected to serve as the prin-ciple officer of justice in their jurisdiction. The story we had to tell was about how one man and his family had fallen victim to a system plagued by racial injustice—a system we're all responsible for as voters, taxpay-ers, and fellow citizens. It changed the tone of the conversation to have an older white Southerner telling that story and asking his neighbors to get involved. We knew that ultimately we'd have to win in court to free John. But we also knew we were beginning to win something even bigger when the conversation on the streets of Wilson shifted to one about justice and the common good.

Often, advocacy for wrongfully convicted black folks in the South had been about trying to win the case by proving that the officers or the prosecutors were racists. Lawyers poured over tapes, testimony, and jury-selection notes for evidence of the N-word or other stereotypes that might "prove" what was obviously the case—that Southern justice is not (nor has it ever been) equally applied. Sometimes they found something and someone got off. Often they did not. But this approach failed to challenge the fundamental immorality of a system that criminalizes a group of people, permanently assigning them to underclass status by means of the law.

We started noting the great exception clause in the Thirteenth Amendment to the US Constitution. It abolished slavery "except as punishment for a crime." We taught our white and Latino allies about the history of convict leasing, whereby white plantation owners had cooperated with local law enforcement throughout the South to arrest former slaves for "vagrancy," then put them back to work, sometimes on the very same plantations where they had earlier been slaves.[3] If convict leasing was a legal means of continuing slavery in the twentieth century, then the so-called War on Drugs has been the legal means of extending second-class citizenship for African Americans into the twenty-first century.[4] Although African Americans constituted less than a quarter of the population of our state, they accounted for more than half of our prison population. What's more, since the birth of the Southern Strategy in the 1970s, the number of North Carolina's prisons had grown nearly sevenfold. A case like John McNeil's, as offensive as it was, turned out to not be an exception, but rather an example of the rule: the single American institution exerting the greatest impact on African American males in the twenty-first century was America's criminal justice system.

One of our coalition partners, People of Faith Against the Death Penalty, pointed out how this dynamic was perhaps most visible in the way North Carolina practiced capital punishment. They had done their homework and crunched the numbers to show that one of the greatest risk factors for receiving a capital sentence in North Carolina's courts was the color of your skin. And perhaps even more telling: the single greatest risk factor was if the victim was white. Black folks accused of killing white people could still be legally lynched.

Such a thing could only happen at great cost to all of us. For decades, so-called conservatives had criminalized a whole class of people—black males—and had filled the state's prisons and created an industry of building new ones, all at the taxpayers' expense. The racially disparate death penalty was costing the state an extra $11 million per year because of the difference in cost between executing a convicted murderer and imprisoning him for life.[5] And the same legislators who were defending capital punishment were telling our coalition members that the state did not have money to expand access to health care, education, and other basic services.

One coalition member confessed that this comprehensive analysis of our criminal justice system was news to him. A white man from rural North Carolina, he noted that his uncle, a retired sheriff's deputy, had killed a young man in cold blood after an argument by the roadside. Though convicted of manslaughter, he never served a single day in jail or prison. Meanwhile, John McNeil would sit in a Georgia prison for six years before we were finally able to gain his freedom.

As we progressed, something powerful was happening. We were learning firsthand the intersections among our coalition partners' issues. Ultimately, whatever affected any one of us directly touched all of us indirectly. In 2009, our coalition lobbied the North Carolina legislature for passage of the Racial Justice Act and saw it pass. It guarantees an appeal to every death row inmate who has been the victim of racial bias in his sentencing. This historic law didn't require proving that the prosecutor was racist. It allowed for statistical evidence of racially disparate sentences, helping a judge see the patterns that had prevailed for decades in Southern justice. Whether Republican or Democrat, every judge who heard evidence presented for a Racial Justice Act appeal commuted the inmate's sentence to life. The data were just that clear.

By themselves, the victories of passing the Racial Justice Act and gaining John McNeil's freedom did not overturn our deeply broken criminal justice system any more than our Smithfield victory had ushered in a new economy. They were both hard-fought battles that only gained us a little ground. But for a coalition trying to learn fusion politics in the twenty-first century, these struggles were our boot camp. They were the fields in which we tested our mettle and learned our weak spots. More important, they gave us the intense conversations and long nights in which diverse groups of people learned to trust one another. Looking back, those years are summed up for me in the words of that evangelical hymn that says, "Just as I am / though tossed about / by many a conflict, / many a doubt." We were not a coalition of angels, but a cross-section of North Carolina residents who had inherited its history of strife and division. Just as we were, we had come together. By pushing forward together, we were learning to see new possibilities. But we were also learning how to trust one another and a Higher Power beyond us when we faced uncertainty.

Though we were gaining cultural power and building our coalition through those early years, the opposition poured money into their well-established machine and took hold of the statehouse in 2010. So even as we worked from our base up, learning to see how our different justice issues intersected and connected, we also had to learn how to be nimble and respond to reactionary attacks. Such is the nature of battle: you don't always get to choose which fronts you're going to focus on. As it happened, the extremists helped us once again. Nothing could have crystallized our vision of the reconstruction we needed so well as the deconstruction they began to enact in 2010.

Because we had followed the money pouring into North Carolina for the 2010 campaigns, we knew their strategy focused on two fronts: the legislature, where they could control the state budget, and the school board of Wake County, where our state capital is located. After winning a majority of the school board seats, extremists immediately set out to dismantle one of the most thoroughly integrated public school systems in the South. Since desegregation, school leaders in Wake County had worked to ensure not only racial diversity but also socioeconomic diversity in every school. Beginning in 2000, Wake leaders had established a goal of an effective, safe learning environment for every child through an enhanced diversity plan. They stipulated that no more than 40 percent of students at a given school should be eligible for free and reduced lunch; no more than 25 percent of students should have scored below grade level on statewide reading tests; and school facilities should operate at between 85 and 115 percent of capacity (that is, within a reasonable range of the size they were built to serve). A decade of data proved that the enhanced diversity policy had worked. Wake County public schools were a regional model for public education.

The anti-diversity extremists who joined the school board in 2010 tried to frame their efforts as a push for "excellence." They said that they wanted better schools for Wake County's kids and that the way to do this was to privatize the public schools. They wanted to frame the debate as a conflict between two different philosophies of education. But we knew that the forces behind their efforts had not believed in public education since the *Brown* decision in 1954. They were continuing a fight that had been going on for half a century to deny a good education to poor people by clustering them in separate, subquality schools.

Some of the big money behind the campaign to privatize Wake County's schools came from Charles and David Koch. Folks who didn't know the history of the freedom movement thought that the Kochs were simply investing personal money in their political and educational philosophy. But we knew there was more to this story. Charles and David were the sons of Freddy Koch, who had tried to have Chief Justice Earl Warren impeached after the unanimous *Brown* decision, which declared "separate but equal" schools unlawful in America. Right here in

North Carolina, over half a century later, they were conspiring with Art Pope and Robert Luddy, a private-school owner, to make Wake County a test case for resegregation through the privatization of public education—all of this in the name of "excellence."

Once again, our job was to shift the public conversation by exposing the extremism. We did our homework: we gathered data on the Wake County diversity plan's results, ran the numbers to compare costs, connected the dots between the public advocates for so-called "neighborhood schools" and their behind-the-scenes funders. We held community forums to educate people and signed up to speak at public school board meetings. Our experiences in Wake County taught us something important about the nature of extremism. If you keep the truth in front of extremists, they will always fall back on brute force. Because they could not answer our moral challenge, they banned us from their meetings. Like Bull Connor in Birmingham, they set the perfect stage for civil disobedience.

In any nonviolent struggle, civil disobedience is a tactic that must be employed strategically. Dr. King learned from Gandhi and taught the civil rights movement the basic, four-stage process that leads to effective civil disobedience. First, a campaign against injustice must do its homework and gather the facts. Second, we attempt to negotiate with the ruling authorities. Only after they've refused us can we move to stage three: self-purification. Because civil disobedience is a decision to personally embrace the suffering we have sought to prevent, it is not simply a strategic opportunity. The opposition may open the door, but we must always be sure we have prepared ourselves before we step through it. Only then, after examining our own willingness to suffer until enemies become friends, can we move to stage four: direct action.[6] In Wake County, our fusion coalition discerned for the first time that civil disobedience was our next step.

When we took over the chambers of the Wake County Board of Education, refusing to leave until we were heard, we knew we were taking our moral case to the broader court of public opinion. Before the people of Wake County heard us, they would see us. So it mattered what we looked like. I stood alongside my white sister, the Reverend Nancy Petty of the Pullen Memorial Baptist Church—a black man in his ministerial robes beside a white woman in hers. Hand in hand beside us were Professor Timothy Tyson, the white chairman of the education committee for North Carolina's NAACP, and Mary Williams, a black woman with the voice of an angel who led us in singing, until they carried us, in handcuffs, off to jail—where we sang some more. Together, our group presented a vivid image of the kind of diverse schools we were arguing for. The local police only reinforced our point when they accidentally tried to arrest the only black member of the school board in the midst of the confusion.

Of course, many said our action was unnecessary—that we were wasting taxpayers' money and police officers' time. But their objections gave us the opportunity to explain the steps we had taken. We didn't want to have to resort to civil disobedience. This was costing us, too, we noted: long nights in jail, lawyers volunteering their time, supporters contributing to post our bail. But we had counted the cost and decided that our children's future was worth it. The question before Wake County, we said, was whether they believed the same.

Meanwhile, as we made our case to the people of Wake County, we were also watching the extremists' attack on another front: the state legislature. Whereas Wake County was a small experiment in what can be deconstructed through a local school board, the 2010 General Assembly was the extremists' real testing ground. Thom Tillis, the speaker of the house, was a board member of the American Legislative Exchange Council (ALEC), through which the Kochs, Art Pope, and other heirs of the Southern Strategy had funded the development of "model legislation" to remake America from its statehouses up. A majority in the General Assembly afforded the extremists an opportunity to begin playing this agenda against Democratic governor Bev Purdue.

On the issue of education, we saw how the attempted takeover of the school board in Wake County fit with their broader agenda when they presented their budget in 2011. Claiming a deficit as their justification, they proposed cutting public school funding so severely that North Carolina would drop to forty-ninth in the ranking of states for the percentage of public funds devoted to our children's education. Though they claimed to be committed to "excellence" in Wake County, they were maneuvering to prove that public schools weren't working by ensuring that they couldn't afford to. After creating a disaster by defunding schools they didn't like, they hoped to redirect public money to private, resegregated schools. Their agenda was evident in the fact that John Tedesco, ringleader of the extremist-controlled Wake County School Board, was running for superintendent of the state board of education.

We took the facts about funding to the General Assembly, reminding them that the North Carolina state constitution guarantees that "the people have a right to the privilege of education, and it is the duty of the State to guard and maintain that right."[7] Each and every legislator in that General Assembly, whether Republican, Democrat, or independent, had sworn to uphold that constitution, placing his or her hand on a Bible, in which the prophet Isaiah says, "Woe to those who make unjust laws."[8] This wasn't merely a political issue. It was a constitutional issue. It was a moral issue. We insisted that it was time to stand up and change the conversation.

As in Wake County, the extremists refused to negotiate. We knew this opened the door for direct action to interrupt and expose their immoral agenda. But we also knew that public opinion wasn't their only pressure point. Civil disobedience might, in fact, push them on one front to act without due and necessary caution on another. As we prepared to take the moral case to the public, our lawyers were waiting for Tillis and his fellow extremists to commit themselves to an unconstitutional attack on public education.

When their immoral budget had been brought to the floor of the house for debate, our coalition partners filled the observation balcony. I stood from my seat to ask Speaker Tillis one question—a question the prophet Micah had asked millennia before me: "What doth the

LORD require?" Given their disregard for the basic tenets of Scripture, we thought it fair to assume that Tillis and others in the chamber might not have read their Bibles. So we offered a brief Bible study in the house chambers, answering the prophet's question in unison: "Do justice, Love mercy, Walk humbly with your God." Having learned the pedagogical efficacy of repetition in North Carolina's public schools, we continued our call-and-response refrain until we were escorted out of the chambers by security officers.

In the hallway I overheard Speaker Tillis telling a reporter he would be happy to meet with anyone who treated *his* house with respect. His reaction was already reflecting the overreach we had hoped to expose. This was, after all, the people's house. Hubris made it difficult for Speaker Tillis to remember that he had been elected to serve us.

As we stood there waiting for the officers to decide what they were going to do with us, one of them pulled out an extra-large set of handcuffs and said to me, "I bought these five months ago for you." He cuffed my hands behind my back and told me to walk down the stairs. But I wasn't about to walk down a flight of stairs with my hands behind my back, led by a man who'd just told me he had been plotting this arrest for months. I told him I preferred to take the elevator, so he led the Reverend T. Anthony Spearman and me together to an elevator. All the way, our supporters were chanting, "Fund education, not incarceration!"

When the doors of the elevator had closed, one of the arresting officers, a young white man, said out loud to his colleague, "We're going to hell for this."

I smiled and said, "That's right, somebody's goin' to hell for what they're doing in this place." Then I closed my eyes, looked up and prayed, *Lord, prove yourself.*

The elevator doors opened and we were on the same floor. Energized to see us again, the crowd chanted all the louder, "Fund education, not incarceration!" As that officer jabbed at the button panel, I whispered just loud enough for him to overhear, *Lord, prove yourself.*

The doors closed, but then opened once again on the same floor.

Those officers were looking terribly nervous. My pastoral instincts told me they might be ready to come down to the altar and confess all their sins. So I said, "Reverend Spearman, please ask the Lord to release this elevator." He prayed aloud in his sonorous baritone, "In the name of Jesus, be thou released."

With that, the elevator went directly to the first floor. As we were getting out, that white officer who looked like he'd seen a ghost whispered to me, "I really don't want be doing this." He put me in the transport vehicle and, when no one else was looking, took the handcuffs off. We spent that night in jail, but the Reverend Spearman and I had fun telling the others that story.

It turned out that the fear of the Lord got into more than just that one officer around the issue of public education. After the General Assembly passed its draconian budget, our coalition's lawyers sued and won an injunction against the budget cuts that would have eliminated pre-kindergarten for thousands of poor children. Judge Howard Manning was clear in his ruling: "Simply put," he said, "it is the duty of the State of North Carolina to protect each and every one of these at-risk and defenseless children, and to provide them their lawful opportunity . . . to take advantage of their equal opportunity to obtain a sound basic education as guaranteed by the North Carolina constitution." The court's clarity on this matter helped the public understand what was at stake. In the elections that fall, the extremists lost their majority on the Wake County School Board. And Tedesco lost his run for superintendent of North Carolina's schools.

We had risked the reputation of our moral movement by choosing to escalate our struggle through civil disobedience, and the increased intensity had stretched us as a coalition. But we were learning together that the old organizer's playbook doesn't always have the answer we need for a new moment. Saul Alinsky and his community organizing tradition had shown us the importance of building power and only tackling "winnable issues." His power analysis was crucial as we considered tactics and timing. But the moral power of standing by that which is good and right could not always be easily calculated beforehand. We hadn't known how long it would take to win on public education. But we had known we were right. So we had pressed forward.

Sometimes, we were learning, we had to hold hands and walk forward into the darkness, even when we didn't know what the next step would bring. Walking by faith wasn't easy. But it was taking us places where the rules of organizing had not allowed us to go. No one knew just what we were becoming, but we knew one thing for sure: there was no turning back.

ultraconserative

CHAPTER 7

The Darkness Before the Dawn

THOUGH WE HAD SEEN important wins in the Smithfield struggle—
in John McNeil's case, in the passing of the Racial Justice Act, the Wake
County struggle, and the court's defense of public education—we knew
the extremists were holding their ground in their most important victory. After taking the General Assembly in 2010, they had acted immediately to redraw voting districts. It was simple power politics, which
Democrats had engaged in as much as Republicans in the past. Only
this time, we were learning, ultraconservative extremists had leveraged
obscene amounts of money to buy a degree of control that they imagined no one could challenge. We would have to sue and wait for years
to get the whole story, but eventually the truth came to light. North
Carolina, it turned out, was ground zero for a coordinated buyout of
American democracy by so-called dark money.

The *Citizens United* decision, we knew, had opened the door for
new kinds of money to pour into America's elections. But the
decision also made it much more difficult to follow the money and see
just where the moneyed elites were focusing their energies. We had our
suspicions, of course. But facts matter in any public debate. Those who
confront power without hard facts will always be accused of touting conspiracy theories.

83

Those who pay attention to human nature, however, need not be naïve about our tendency to conspire. The prophet Jeremiah said four thousand years ago, "The heart is deceitful above all things, and desperately corrupt; who can understand it?"[1] Power plus secrecy guarantees conspiracy in human affairs. The authors of North Carolina's constitution understood this. In order to preserve an open, democratic process in our state, they guaranteed every citizen the right to "assemble together to consult for their common good, to instruct their representatives, and to apply to the General Assembly for redress of grievances." This is the right of every North Carolinian, regardless of race, creed, or class. But because this right had been trampled during the nineteenth century in the secret, closed-door meetings of white power elites, the wise authors of our constitution had followed this democratic guarantee immediately with a strict prohibition: "but secret political societies are dangerous to the liberties of a free people and shall not be tolerated."[2]

"Secret political societies," we learned, were precisely the enemy we were up against. Immediately following their heavily financed victory in 2010, extremists controlling the General Assembly used their previously dormant State Government Leadership Foundation (SGLF) to hire an outside consultant, Tom Hofeller, to oversee the gerrymandering of North Carolina's voting districts. Because the IRS does not require the SGLF to disclose information about its donors, it provided the perfect shroud behind which Art Pope and his allies could fortify themselves against all future challenges. Their strategy was simple: identify those who would vote against them, isolate those votes in a minority of "packed" districts, and thus guarantee "democratic" power through a majority of sympathetic districts. Henceforth and forevermore, they thought, the popular vote wouldn't matter. A majority of North Carolinians could vote against them but they would still maintain power by winning a majority of the districts.

The General Assembly leadership, whose campaigns Pope had funded, assigned him as "special counsel" to the redistricting team, thereby protecting him from subpoena through attorney-client privilege.

You don't have to be a conspiracy theorist to see the level of conspiring behind this plan. The same man who had bought the legislature was paying the consultant who was working side by side with him, all under carefully arranged conditions designed to keep the public from connecting the dots. One layer after another, the extremists tried to cover up what they knew they could only do in secret.[3]

If any of them had been listening when they made their obligatory public appearances at church, they might have heard these words of Jesus: "Nothing is covered up that will not be revealed, or hidden that will not be known. Therefore whatever you have said in the dark shall be heard in the light, and what you have whispered in private rooms shall be proclaimed upon the housetops."[4] As our coalition filed lawsuits and fought in court to expose this conspiracy against the people of North Carolina, we held on to the promise that a lie cannot live forever. But we knew that this was not the narrative folks were reading in their newspapers or watching on the evening news. When the extremists came out from behind the curtains of their secret societies, they smiled, shook hands and kissed babies. To most people, it looked like they were good, honest businessmen using their skills to help North Carolina recover from the Great Recession.

Once again, we knew our job was to change the public narrative. If all folks heard in the public conversation was spin about how the economy was rebounding and unemployment rates were going down, they were damned to blaming themselves for their own suffering. *Everyone else is doing better*, poor people would tell themselves. *We must be doing something wrong.*

But we knew the extremists' narrative about economic recovery was little more than a smoke screen for their obsessive pursuit of total control. Gar Alperovitz, a political economist at the University of Maryland, offered a penetrating analysis of the "silent depression" that had caught up with us. "What we're really beginning to experience is a process of slow decay, punctuated by a recurring economic crisis, one in which reforms achieve only sporadic gains," he wrote in *America Beyond*

Capitalism. Analyzing trends over time, across Republican and Demo-cratic administrations, he noted how

> growing inequality, economic dislocation, failing democratic ac-countability, deepening poverty, ecological degradation, greater inva-sions of liberty and growing imprisonment, especially of minorities, continue to slowly and quietly challenge the belief in the capacities and moral integrity of the overall system of the governing elite.[5]

His analytical summary was, almost item by item, a catalogue of the cries we'd heard from our coalition partners. The challenge was how to overcome the spin of the governing elite and make poverty personal in the public square.

Several coalition partners came together at the beginning of 2012 and announced that we would host a "Putting a Face on Poverty" tour, because in both our private and public politics, many Americans had become accustomed to committing attention violence against the poor. Like the religious leaders in Jesus's parable of the Good Samaritan, too many in our society had made it a habit to cross to the other side of the road and ignore the man holding a "will work for food" sign who has been beaten up by an economic system that thinks it does not need him. In both private and public attitudes—even in pulpits and places of worship—concern for the vulnerable was not visible. Ours was a tour designed to change the way North Carolina thought and talked about the economy.

Nearly 1.6 million of God's human family, we pointed out, were living in abject poverty in North Carolina.[6] As we traveled the back roads of North Carolina, one of American poverty's native homes, Gene Nichol of the University of North Carolina's Center on Poverty, Work, and Opportunity pointed out the irony of the fact that here, where we have the most poor people in the land, we also had the most political leaders who were utterly untroubled by it. Ten of the country's poorest twelve states were Southern. Though about 15 percent of Americans lived in poverty generally, in Mississippi it was 23 percent; Louisiana,

22 percent; Arkansas, 20 percent; Georgia, 19.1 percent; South Carolina, 19 percent; Texas, 19 percent.

North Carolina came in close to the bottom of the list, but we joined the other former Confederate states to set the gold standard for American economic deprivation. In North Carolina, 18 percent of us were officially poor—over 25 percent of our children and more than 40 percent of our children of color. This was the reality that we wanted to help the people of North Carolina see. In one of the most economically potent states of the strongest nation on earth, over 40 percent of our kids of color were living in wrenching poverty.

What's more, under the extremist leadership that was claiming an economic rebound, North Carolina had one of the country's fastest rising poverty rates. A decade before, in the 2000s, we had been twenty-sixth from the bottom—a little better than average. But we were down to twelfth from the bottom, speeding past the competition. Two million of us were classified by the federal government as hungry—over 20 percent, the nation's fourth-highest rate. Nearly 622,000 of our kids were going to bed hungry each night.

Who were these people? And why didn't we know their names and their stories? That was the basic question behind our poverty tour. We invited journalists and students, pastors and community leaders to join us on four separate trips through each quadrant of our state.

In Henderson County we met an optimistic yet tearful young woman who had been stricken with diabetes. She wanted to marry the good man she loved, who would help her raise her daughter. But she told us she couldn't. If she did, she would lose her Medicaid insurance. Without it, she worried, she might lose her life.

We visited with the hundreds of clients of the Beloved Community Center in Greensboro. We talked to Greg and Sammy, Leona and Kay—black and white folks who were homeless, living in extreme poverty. Many of them lined up at three in the morning to get a shower when the doors opened at six thirty. Four had recently died on the streets in a single week.

Just down the road, at Greensboro Urban Ministries, five hundred meals were served, three times a day, seven days a week, to the hungry and destitute. Still, they said they couldn't meet the demand in a city where poverty was supposedly not a problem.

We met and talked to a fifty-seven-year-old man in Reidsville who was living in a storm drain. It wasn't the ideal situation, he confessed, but it at least helped him stay out of the elements. He had been laid off after a plant closure, having worked thirty-eight years. In thirty-six months of homelessness, he told us he'd been hungry every single day. The "trickle down," he reported, "never seems to trickle on us."

One day on the tour we came to Hickory, North Carolina, where we were invited to walk down a path into the woods. There we witnessed the fresh reality of man's inhumanity to man. As we walked along the path, we saw baby dolls and toys, eerie signs that there were children living under the cover of trees and bushes in the woods. This is what an "economic recovery" looked like for nearly a fifth of our state—people forced to live like animals in the richest nation ever to exist.

When we got to the community in the middle of the woods, we met God's family—black, white and brown, male and female, young and old. I was brought to uncontrollable tears when our new friends welcomed us. They swept the dirt and made space for us among the grass and the weeds. They told us how the authorities would often come out to their small community and run them out of the woods because the city did not want to acknowledge its level of devastating poverty. "But we wanted you to come, Reverend Barber," a woman said to me as she held my hand. "It might mean we lose everything we've got, but we wanted you to come so somebody might at least know we're here."

These were the moral witnesses we needed to help us stand against the extremist takeover of our statehouse. Our coalition had learned how essential it is to a fusion movement for those most directly affected to speak for themselves. But no one was listening to poor people. Republicans and Democrats alike were struggling to prove that their program was the best way to lift the middle class. Justice organizations created a platform for people of color, women, labor, the environment, and

LGBTQ folk. But no one was handing a microphone to poor people. The way to beat mystery money and the secret conspiracies of the governing elite was to trust that their evil deeds would come to light as we lifted up the voices of the most vulnerable. As the psalmist had taught Israel to sing through long days of exile, "The stone which the builders rejected has become the head of the corner."[7] We did not know the extent of the gap our coalition would have to span, but we had stumbled upon the architectural insight which would ensure our moral arch's stability. The people the builders had rejected were to be the capstone of our coalition.

The year 2012 saw an election. Having put their redistricting plans into place, the extremists were prepared to invest with surgical precision in campaigns to guarantee them the total control they longed for. Their new maps told them exactly where they had to win. But money, they feared, wouldn't be enough to seal their victory. In the end, they could only invest in particular candidates, none of whom were particularly compelling. Like King Herod at the time of Jesus' birth, they were scared to death that after all of their conspiring they wouldn't be able to manipulate the people of North Carolina.

So they did what implementing the Southern Strategy had trained them to do: they moved to stir up the fear that would most likely divide poor people who were waking up to the fact that the extremists' "economic recovery" wasn't doing anything for them. For so much of Southern history, the fear of black people—especially the fear of black men threatening white women—had been enough to divide and conquer poor people along race lines. The extremists had tried to tap this old fear in their 2010 takeover, direct-mailing flyers insinuating that the Racial Justice Act was going to put dangerous black men back in white folks' neighborhoods. (In an ironic twist of fate, they used the image of Henry McCollum as an example of a dangerous black man; yet McCollum, an inmate on North Carolina's death row, was later exonerated by the work of North Carolina's Innocence Commission and officially pardoned by the governor.) But our moral fusion coalition had demonstrated clearly that black, white, and brown were going to stand together in North Carolina. So they moved to exploit a new fear, but cloaked it in moral language about the "defense of marriage."

Their ploy was to get out the vote in the 2012 primary by putting a constitutional amendment on the ballot banning gay marriage in North Carolina. A judge eventually forced the National Organization for Marriage, which was intimately involved in this strategy, to turn over internal documents which revealed that their goal had little to do with morality. They had pitched this so-called "Amendment One" as a way to split North Carolina's growing black vote, pointing out that many African Americans were religious conservatives and would not support gay marriage. The way to split a moral movement, they said, is to get them arguing about morality.

Many so-called conservative Christians, black and white, were galvanized by the buzzwords they had been taught to fear and joined the crusade against gay folk. Franklin Graham, son of the ailing Billy Graham, who had long been North Carolina's most famous preacher and moral authority, used both his father's name and the money that had been given to support his father's evangelism ministry to run ads in support of the amendment. Dr. William C. Martin of Rice University, who had written a glowing biography of Billy Graham, immediately asked whether the ads could have actually come from the man he'd written about. "After realizing that he'd been cynically manipulated by Richard Nixon," Dr. Martin noted, "Billy Graham resisted joining the Religious Right." Dr. Graham had seen through the Southern Strategy from the very beginning and did not support its aims. Evidently, he had not been able to pass this political insight on to his son.

Though we didn't have much time, we knew that the integrity of our coalition, which had included LGBTQ sisters and brothers from the beginning, depended upon answering the challenge of Amendment One with moral clarity. Like the Pharisees who tried to trap Jesus by means of the old political divisions of established camps, the extremists had posed a question designed to divide our ranks by casting doubt either among the LGBTQ community or among the African American community about whether our moral movement truly represented them. I recognized the trap and decided to trust what Jesus had told his disciples: "When they bring you before . . . the rulers and the authorities, do not be anxious how or what you are to answer or what you are to say; for the Holy Spirit will teach you in that very hour what you ought to say."[8]

I looked back at the history of the NAACP and recalled that during the civil rights movement, when white folks had tried to make it illegal for white and black folks to marry across the color line, the NAACP had not endorsed biracial marriage. They had, instead, recognized that the effort to restrict someone's right to marry the person they choose was a fear-based tactic to establish hate as law. The NAACP had opposed these bans not because their coalition endorsed biracial marriage, but because they endorsed the moral and constitutional principle of equal protection under the law.

Against a similar fear-based tactic, our movement's position had to be the same. It wasn't our job to endorse same-sex marriage. After all, we had never had to endorse heterosexual marriage or partners living together outside of marriage. As a pastor, I had counseled scores of people on these deeply personal matters, knowing that the church had ordained me to pass on its wisdom about how to live well as sexual beings in human community. But as a pastor, I also knew that the US Constitution's First Amendment, guaranteeing religious freedom, protected the right of every church, synagogue, and mosque to discern together what God's definition of marriage is. Our First Amendment right entailed freedom from any government attempt to tell us what God says about marriage.

But the fundamental principle of equal protection under the law was a constitutional and moral principle which our movement had not only to endorse but also to defend. In the end, it didn't matter whether my faith tradition told me marriage was to be between one man and one woman; all of our faiths made clear that the codification of hate is never righteous. Legalized discrimination is never just. And a moral fusion movement cannot be divided by the fear-based tactics of so-called conservatives.

Other ministers and I made the rounds to church meetings through-out our state, especially among the black churches that extremist organizers had targeted with campaign propaganda. We learned quickly that once we were able to reframe the issue, people quickly grasped how the treatment of LGBTQ citizens was an issue of civil rights and human rights. Our message only lacked reach. Amendment One passed before we could get to all of North Carolina's rural communities. But in the places where we were able to reframe the issue, the results were clear: voters in majority-black precincts in North Carolina's five major cities rejected the amendment. In Durham, where our NAACP office is located, not a single majority-black precinct supported the amendment. It failed by a ratio of two to one on the African American side of Scotland Neck, a rural community in Halifax County, where our movement had established a strong base by organizing against environ-mental racism.

Within two years, Amendment One was struck down by the courts, bringing marriage equality to North Carolina long before most in the LBGTQ community could have imagined. But we knew in 2012 that Amendment One was a smoke screen; it was never about defending mar-riage. It was about protecting extremists' power by playing on fear to get people to vote against their own interests and to drive a wedge between potential allies. Added on top of their long-term strategy of dark money investment and gerrymandered districts, Amendment One was a divide-and-conquer tactic to complete the extremist take-over of North Caro-lina's state government. And it worked. The year 2013 marked the first time since 1896 that Republicans held total, unchecked power in both the legislature and the governor's office. Back then, the Republicans had been united with Populists in North Carolina's first fusion coalition. But these twenty-first-century extremists who called themselves Republican had drunk the Tea Party's tea and sniffed some mighty strong Koch to complete the takeover they'd been plotting for decades. North Carolina was about to witness the full force of their extremism.

In many ways, that long winter of 2012–13 was our darkest hour.

As we prepared for our seventh coalition People's Assembly in Raleigh that February, we knew the avalanche of corporately funded extremism which had poured into North Carolina since 2008 was a reaction against the perceived threat of our coalition's power. From 16 organizations that had gathered five thousand people in 2007 we'd grown to a coalition of 145 organizations representing black, white, and brown, labor and civil rights organizations, doctors and the uninsured, businesspeople and the unemployed, women and men, gay and straight, young and old, documented and undocumented. Standing together against one attack after another, our ranks had grown fourfold, bringing as many people to Raleigh each winter as Dr. King had brought to Selma when he put out a national call for solidarity after Bloody Sunday in 1965. Our indigenously led, state-government-focused moral fusion coalition had scared the hell out of the governing elite. We knew before we started that the same forces in North Carolina's history had orchestrated America's only coup d'état, in 1898. Seven years of experience showed us that, although time had changed the elite's weapons, it had not moderated their extremism.

But a century of reflection and seven years of fusionist organizing had taught us some important lessons about who we were. When we gathered in Raleigh that winter, I talked to our twenty thousand battle-weary foot soldiers about the importance of knowing who we are in times like these. The greatest threat to our coalition was not the power of our opposition. They could threaten us. They could hurt us. They might, in their blind hubris, even try to kill some of us. But they could not, in the end, deny us. Because ours was a moral struggle, we knew we would win if we didn't give up.

The only question was how long the fight would go on—which was why the greatest threat to our coalition was the temptation to forget what we had learned about our identity. A nonviolent struggle has two possible ends: winning the opposition as friends or giving up the battle. Though our coalition included the full spectrum of North Carolina's diversity, we had come to recognize a common vision for our future in the history of the South's antiracist freedom movement. Our relationships with one another were not simply transactional—a means to achieve our various organization's goals. They had become transformational, lifting each of us to a new understanding of our interconnectedness as human beings and living members of one family. None of us would be free until all of us were free. Thus, the slave's anthem became a battle cry even for the daughters and sons of former slave owners: "Before I'd be a slave / I'll be buried in my grave / and go home to my Lord / and be free."

The self-knowledge that allowed each of us to sing an old slave song was what we could not forget. For as long as we identified with the oppressed and excluded, we could not be distracted or bought off. The stone that the builders rejected had, indeed, become our capstone. However long the distances between us, the magnitude of our chasms of division, we could trust that that arch would hold so long as we kept the rejected at the center. They had, after all, been our guiding light for generations. With far less resources than we had at our disposal, Harriet Tubman had joined hands with her Quaker friends and organized. Long before e-mail blasts, J. W. Hood and Samuel Stanford Ashley had pressed their way to Raleigh and come together. When folks still thought tweeting was just something birds do, Ella Baker taught our brother Bob Zellner and his SNCC friends how to sit in, stand up, and register voters. The moral arch we'd been grafted onto might be long, but we knew which way it bent. If we could just remember that we were called together as repairers of the breach, we would make it to the other side.

It was the slave's song that could help us remember who we were. This insight, I realized, was rooted in the spirituality that my grandmamma had passed down to me—a faith she had inherited from the children and grandchildren of slaves. And it was the songs my mother played on the piano in that hospital lobby that had sustained me through my own dark night of the soul. In our collective dark night, the movement was learning the same lesson. As I'd traveled the state, often speaking four and five times a day on three hours of sleep, a woman named Yara Allen kept showing up at rallies and events. She would stand and lead the people in singing. She wasn't a performer, but a song leader, and something in her songs steeled my soul. They whispered to me, "Hold on, just a little while longer."

The Bible tells us that the prophet Elisha once called for a minstrel, and after the minstrel's song, "the hand of the LORD came upon him."[9] Yara Allen's songs had the same effect on us. When she led us in singing those freedom songs, we knew who we were. As long as we kept singing, it didn't matter how long the extremists' attacks lasted. We would keep standing. We would keep fighting. We would keep pushing forward together, not one step back.

CHAPTER 8

A Moral Movement
for the Nation

WITH NO POLITICAL OPPOSITION to check their power, the extremists in North Carolina joined hands to remake our state in 2013. In their minds, it was the perfect test case for the comprehensive blueprint ALEC had developed. Thom Tillis, a former ALEC board member, was speaker of the North Carolina House. Phil Berger, an ultraconservative, was leading the state senate. And Pat McCrory had just been elected governor with the full support of Art Pope's extremist machine. As an indication of just how deeply aligned with the extremism he was, McCrory appointed Pope the state budget director. The man who had both plotted and funded this twenty-first-century coup was now controlling North Carolina's purse strings.

It didn't take long for this quadrumvirate to put its cards on the table. They introduced legislation to block the expansion of Medicaid to half a million North Carolinians and cut off federal unemployment benefits for 170,000 of our unemployed sisters and brothers. Echoing the interposition of federally mandated integration the 1960s, which led Alabama's Governor George Wallace to block the door of the University of Alabama to African American students, both moves were intended to deny North Carolinians access to federal benefits they had already been granted. The very politicians who had campaigned for an "economic comeback" were blocking the flow of millions of dollars into our state's economy on ideological grounds.

But they didn't stop there. They introduced a bill to overturn our Racial Justice Act. They moved to end public financing for judicial elections (which would allow them to buy off judges to influence them to refuse our challenges to their unconstitutional actions in court). They wrote a new tax code for the state, throwing out the earned-income tax credit (which helped nearly a million working families) while impoverishing the state by slashing taxes for the most wealthy. They introduced a bill that would allow people to buy guns without a permit and carry them in public parks and restaurants.

But they didn't stop there, either. There was, after all, no political foe to stop them from unleashing every fear they had stoked and each division they'd leveraged into a wedge issue. When Mr. Pope's budget was presented to the General Assembly, it included the same unconstitutional cuts to pre-K education against which we had won an injunction in court. What's more, Pope's budget proposed shifting $90 million of public funds to private schools through vouchers. At a stroke it eliminated entire state-funded agencies, such as Legal Aid, that provide constitutionally protected legal assistance to prisoners. Meanwhile, it proposed raises for the so-called conservatives Governor McCrory had hired to oversee North Carolina's economic "comeback."

Finally, on top of this full slate of extremist legislation, they introduced their "monster" voter-suppression bill during the week of March 9th, when we in the freedom movement remember Bloody Sunday and all those who bled and died for the Voting Rights Act of 1965. We called it a monster bill from the beginning, for two reasons: First, its scope was monstrous, ranging from restrictions that would require a state-issued photo ID (which 318,000 registered voters didn't have) to drastic cuts in early voting. It would eliminate same-day registration, take away the automatic restoration of voting rights for ex-felons, and end the child-dependency tax deduction ($2,000 to $2,500 per child) for parents of college students who chose to vote where they attended school—in effect, a way of punishing the parents via the tax code for their children's exercising the voting franchise. We called it a monster to help people see the hydralike reach of this many-headed effort to suppress votes. But we also had to call it a monster because its obvious intent was as vicious as Bull Connor's dogs in Birmingham and Sheriff Jim Clark's billy clubs on the Edmund Pettus Bridge. By targeting voters who were students, poor people, the elderly, African Americans, and ex-felons, they were admitting that they knew a majority of us would not support their agenda and would try to vote them out of power. Nevertheless, they were going to carry it forward by any means necessary, doing everything in their power to make sure we could never vote them out of power.

We had beaten them back in 2008, when President Obama won North Carolina. But the extremists showed us during our Holy Week of 2013 that they were willing to do anything to make sure we never beat them again.

As a preacher, I saw what was happening in Raleigh that Holy Week through the lens of Jesus bearing his cross. When Jesus led his fusion coalition into Jerusalem that first Holy Week, it was a joyous occasion. Jerusalem greeted him as a king. But the governing elite reacted harshly, playing on dissention within the coalition's ranks to buy off Judas and turn the crowds against Jesus. Just before he hung his head and died, a victim of the very worst that the powers can do to us, Jesus prayed, "Father, forgive them for they know not what they do." He loved his enemies to the very end, the Bible tells us, holding on to the moral center of his campaign, even in the face of death. When he died, the whole world went dark. Even still, a few from his movement held on.

I recalled a story from the Birmingham campaign of 1963, when Dr. King and the Southern Christian Leadership Conference had come in to support the local desegregation effort. The year before, in Albany, Georgia, King had experienced what he considered a defeat in the battle against Police Chief Laurie Pritchett, who studied nonviolent tactics and concluded that the best way to diffuse them is to meet them nonviolently, avoiding the extremism that gives protestors the moral high ground. By refusing to get angry or react violently in public, Pritchett had avoided media attention and subverted King's plan to integrate Albany by drawing outside attention to a violent confrontation.

But Birmingham's Bull Connor had a record of extremism. If the movement pushed him hard enough, they knew he would expose the ugliness of Jim Crow. And they were right. Connor sent out the patrol wagons and arrested everyone the movement could find to march. But still, Birmingham wouldn't budge. Once again it was Holy Week, and Dr. King was preparing to preach the story of Jesus, who had found another way to victory by laying down his life in love. Through the lens of the Easter story, King recognized that a moral movement must press on, even in its darkest hour, trusting the One who can make a way out of no way—believing that we find a way by pressing forward.

Dr. King excused himself from a planning meeting on that Good Friday and, according to his aides, came back wearing denim work clothes. He was dressed for jail. He would march against Connor's orders and get arrested, he said, even though he did not know how it would advance the campaign. He was pressing forward into the darkness, trusting that a power beyond him would shine the light of truth on Birmingham's dark hatred.

THAT EASTER WEEKEND in the Birmingham jail turned out to be Dr. King's most famous direct action against segregation in the South. The letter he wrote from his cell went around the world, inspiring people of conscience and moral movements from South Africa to China. The Birmingham campaign was followed by the Children's March, which grabbed the attention of the nation and precipitated the Civil Rights Act of 1964. But Dr. King didn't know any of that when he decided to go to jail. He only knew that pressing forward in the way of truth, being willing to embrace unearned suffering, was the way of his Lord. He had learned from the great river of the Southern freedom movement that such a "faith act" is sometimes the only way forward.[1]

As the avalanche of extremism continued to dump a mountain of despair on North Carolina fifty years later, our young people showed us that a new "faith act" was needed. When the monster voter-suppression bill came to the floor for debate, college students with duct tape covering their mouths filled the observation area, exposing how this wicked law sought to silence them. When the bill finally passed, on April 25, we knew the students had shown us the way, just as they had back in 1960 when they sat down at the Woolworth lunch counter in Greensboro, refusing to accept Jim Crow's old assumptions. It was time for our faith act. I gathered with a core group of our coalition partners to plan.

We did not have to meet for long. Having journeyed together for seven years, we knew what we had to do. Frankly, it was a meeting not unlike the meetings we'd had for years—meetings we would continue to have, finding our way together. We did not think we were doing anything particularly profound when we decided that, on the following Monday, seventeen of us would exercise our constitutional right to instruct our legislators about the evil they were committing despite the fact that they refused to meet with us. The Reverend T. Anthony Spearman, whose prayer had scared the officer in the elevator two years earlier, was there. Nancy Petty and Tim Tyson, who'd gone to jail with me during the Wake County struggle, were there. Bob Zellner, who had stayed with our movement since winning John McNeil's freedom, was there, too, reminding us what Rosa Parks had whispered in his ear back in Montgomery: "When you see something that's wrong, eventually you have to do something about it." We were a freedom family, doing what we had learned to do. We didn't know where it would lead, but we knew we had to do everything in our power to expose the extremism that had become so normal in the daily news.

We were disappointed but not surprised when the extremists decided to arrest us rather than hear our petition. What did surprise me was the outpouring of support we witnessed as we came out of jail early that next morning. After watching our arrests on the news, hundreds of people called, e-mailed, and even came down to the jail to ask what they could do to help. It seemed as if our small faith act had sent a spark into a powder keg. People who had been silently suffering and quietly concerned suddenly saw our moral witness as a rallying cry. Everyone who called wanted to know when we would be going back to the General Assembly.

So we started to make plans to petition our legislators again the following Monday. We put the word out through our coalition partners and met with people who were willing to be arrested to tell them what we had learned the week prior and offer training in nonviolence. Having worked for years to plan lobby days at the legislature, I admit I was surprised to see that hundreds of people had showed up on Jones Street on only a few days' notice. The second Monday, twice as many people were arrested, as hundreds packed into the statehouse rotunda, singing freedom songs and chanting, "This is what democracy looks like." Our moral movement had touched a nerve. When the thirty-two arrestees were released the next morning, we announced that we would be back again the following week for another "Moral Monday."

On that third Monday, when the number of volunteers willing to risk arrest doubled once again, our crowd packed both floors of the statehouse rotunda, spilling out into hallways and onto porches outside the building. As officers began to arrest our moral witnesses, hundreds moved outside the building, where they found the transport bus that had been sent over to deliver people to jail. At the sight of a sister or brother in handcuffs being led to the bus, the crowd would erupt with shouts of "Thank you!" and "We love you!" Our friends who were being processed out through the building's basement cafeteria said they could hear the roar of the crowd before they even got outside.

Blinded by their own propaganda, the extremists simply couldn't make sense of why thousands of North Carolinians were suddenly rising up in protest against their regime. Because our crowds had outgrown the building, we set up a stage on the mall behind the statehouse the next week, giving folks an hour or so after getting off work at five to gather, sing together, hear the stories of people who were directly affected by our state's extremism, and state clearly the reasons for our moral dissent.

Legislators and their staff came out on the statehouse balconies to observe the open-air People's Assembly that was happening outside their chambers. One Republican state senator, Tom Goolsby, wrote it off as a "Moron Monday" in his local paper back home,[2] but such callous disregard only fueled the media frenzy around this popular uprising. When the time came for our moral witnesses to enter the statehouse, risking arrest, the crowd parted, creating an aisle down the middle. People lifted their hands to bless the scores of sisters and brothers who were laying down their freedom to proclaim to North Carolina that we were under attack.

The media jumped at the scene of thousands of people gathered on the Halifax Mall, improvising a way of being together even as we reflected the multiethnic democracy that America strives to become. If it had happened just once, it would have been a high-water mark in our nation's long march toward freedom. But the incredible thing—the fact that amazed me over and again—was that it kept happening. Word spread, and the crowd kept growing. I went out of state for a meeting at Highlander that had been planned for months, and while I was away, Moral Monday kept growing. Throughout one of the wettest summers on record in North Carolina, thousands of people stood outside their statehouse every Monday evening for thirteen weeks and never got rained on. To the tune of the old spiritual "Wade in the Water," one of our song leaders sang, "Forward together, not one step back / God gonna trouble the waters."

It seemed as if a new kind of revival had taken hold of us, reminiscent of the camp meetings at which people gathered outdoors to hear the message of America's Third Great Awakening in the late nineteenth century, when evangelical preachers made a direct connection between personal salvation and social justice. We improvised a liturgy that was deeply rooted in the lessons of our fusion coalition. Music mattered, so Yara Allen worked closely with the diverse cultural artists who were already committed to the movement to begin each gathering with songs that sang of our struggle. We reworked old freedom songs and improvised new chants on the spot. Watching the arrestees pour out of the building in handcuffs early on, someone shouted, "You're gonna need another bus / 'cause baby there are more of us!" Moral Mondays weren't a stage for artists to perform, but rather a platform from which they could lead us with their gifts. The point of the songs was to knit us together as a new kind of community.

After we joined our voices together in singing, we knew it was important for the crowd to hear from people directly affected by economic hardship and injustice. So this became our testimony time. An unemployed worker would stand up front and tell us what losing unemployment benefits meant to him and his family. A teacher would testify about what budget cuts meant for her and her classroom. A woman who qualified for Medicaid under the Affordable Care Act told us what it feels like to know you can't get treatment for cancer because some politicians in Raleigh are still mad that a black man is in the White House. Week after week, moral witnesses came forward to speak for themselves about how the legislators' extremism was hurting North Carolina. We had learned that these poor and hurting people were the capstone of our moral arch. As it turned out, they were also some of our most compelling speakers. Many who came to a Moral Monday unsure of how they felt about political issues said these testimonies gave them clarity: they knew that laws which so obviously hurt people are wrong and must be challenged.

The platform our fusion coalition had built was one from which poor and hurting people's voices could be heard. They were our featured speakers, and we invited them to share their stories regardless of race, creed, or political affiliation. Of course, once the media frenzy took off, all of those politicians who spend millions of dollars to get their faces on TV couldn't wait to get in front of the cameras. When we told them that our stage wasn't for them, some of them started giving interviews to reporters on the edge of the crowd. I'll never forget one evening, as a registered Republican and a registered Democrat were standing on stage together, talking about how the legislature had cut off their unemployment benefits, I noticed a state legislator giving an interview to the press. As soon as our two unemployed brothers had finished, I stepped to the microphone and asked the whole crowd to help me shame the politician into taking his show somewhere else. We were absolutely clear that anyone was welcome to be part of Moral Mondays, but we were gathered to hear from the people about how our state's extremism was affecting them.

Because we knew that the opposition would fall back on so-called political realism ("You may not like it, but this is simply how it is"), we also knew it was important for the people to hear expert testimony that another way is possible. So, following the testimony of directly affected people each week, we created space in our liturgy for economists, public policy experts, and lawyers to lay out our agenda and explain how it would work. College graduates who came to Moral Mondays said they learned more about government and civil society in those short talks than they had in whole semesters of mandatory civics classes. As the great American pragmatist John Dewey taught us, "learning by doing" is key to internalizing the principles we hold dear as a people. Moral Mondays became a space where a new North Carolina could practice democracy together. We were learning the principles of our state constitution by putting them into practice.

But perhaps the most distinctive mark of Moral Mondays—the focal point of our liturgy that gave the movement its name—was our insistence that, at its heart, our movement have a moral framework. Like the old revival services, each week concluded with a sermon and an altar call, when those who wished to make a new spiritual commitment were invited to come forward publicly. As a Christian preacher from a revivalist tradition, I knew this pattern well. But I was careful to acknowledge that my Holy Bible was not the only holy book. When I or another minister stood to preach, we never stood alone. We stood with Christian, Jewish, and Muslim clerics surrounding us, offering the people a visible sign of the message we were trying to proclaim. Each of us had a tradition we held dear and a message we shared with our flocks on Friday, Saturday, or Sunday. We weren't giving any of that up. But on Monday we were learning to stand together and proclaim the deepest shared values of our faith traditions. We were learning how those values are embedded in our state constitution. And we were experiencing a revival like we'd never seen before—one where the Spirit lifts us all from where we were to higher ground.

I started to share a bit of insight I'd learned from my son, who studied environmental science in college. He told me, "Daddy, if you ever get lost in mountainous terrain, it's important to know that there's something called a snake line. Below the snake line, you might run into a copperhead or a rattlesnake sunning on the rocks of our Blue Ridge Mountains. But if you can get above the snake line, you're safe, because those venomous creatures can't live up there." Moral Mondays were exposing the extremism of venomous politics in our state and helping folk see what dangerous terrain we had gotten ourselves into. But I kept telling them that there was a snake line somewhere on the mountain. If we could just move together toward higher ground, we'd be all right. The important thing was not to give up. The important thing was to keep on climbing. Every week I cried out against the nightmare we were witnessing to hold out the hope of higher ground.

This public proclamation was essential to our liturgy, but it was not the end. Every week when I was finished preaching, I invited people to come forward and make a public profession of their faith in a new North Carolina by exercising their constitutional right to petition their legislators in the General Assembly. They knew, of course, that they were risking arrest. Each person who had decided to make this public witness wore an armband to signify that they'd spent the afternoon doing nonviolence training at a local church. But it was an awe-inspiring sight, week after week, to watch the crowd part and make way for these nonviolent foot soldiers who were ready to sacrifice their own freedom to put our proposed future into practice. A Presbyterian minister from Charlotte, attending his first Moral Monday, said, "Never in my life have I seen the proclaimed Word put on flesh and move into such a direct action." Some of us who'd been doing liturgy all of our lives began to realize its power in the public square.

After the General Assembly adjourned and went home, stubbornly refusing to hear our cries, we scheduled one final Moral Monday in Raleigh, moving our stage from behind the statehouse to Fayetteville Street, Raleigh's Champs-Élysées, on the opposite side of the old state capitol. Nearly a thousand people had gone to jail in a dozen weeks of civil disobedience, marking the largest state-focused direct action campaign in US history. Their commitment had gained the attention of the nation, bringing reporters from national newspapers and cable news networks. The biggest political story in the country wasn't what was happening inside any legislative chambers, but what was happening at these weekly people's assemblies.

Before that rally, where some twenty thousand people gathered to conclude our long summer of discontent in Raleigh, the question the media kept asking was "What difference has all of this protest made?" Their imagination was often so captive to the story they had been telling that they couldn't understand the words we were saying when we told them Moral Mondays weren't a new movement. These protests had not erupted spontaneously as some sort of natural reflex against extremism. They were the fruit of long-term organizing and hard-fought coalition building. We tried over and again to explain how North Carolina's extremism was itself a strategic attack against the fusion coalition that had produced Moral Mondays. But the point was a difficult fit with the twenty-four-hour news cycle. Every time we opened the floor for questions, they wanted to know what difference we were making.

I'd been at this long enough to know that the doubts that are spoken in public are the ones that weigh on the minds of the people—especially of those who had only recently joined our ranks. So I chose as my text for that thirteenth Moral Monday Psalm 118, a beautiful song of ancient Israel that had taught us how the poor and rejected were to be the capstone of our movement. I highlighted what that psalm goes on to say: "This is the LORD's doing; it is marvelous in our eyes. This is the day which the LORD has made; let us rejoice and be glad in it."[3]

Yes, we had seen an avalanche of extremism. Yes, we had a long way to go to undo the cynical attacks of the governing elites. But we could not press on without taking time to celebrate how far we had come. I told those twenty thousand people gathered on Fayetteville Street to take a moment to look around at one another. We were the multiracial democracy that scared the hell out of Southern politicians. Despite the best efforts of their Southern Strategy to divide and conquer us, we had come together.

For every face in that beautiful sea of God's children, there was a story. I recognized members of the teachers union who had, in the early days of our coalition building, thought the HKonJ agenda too broad for all of their members to accept. But our struggle had taught us how the enemy of voting rights is the enemy of education. Now here we were, standing together. I noted the pink shirts of Planned Parenthood members and recalled my early conversations with their president, Janet Colm. I'd told her that with our broad coalition we could not endorse abortion, so she asked, "Can you support women's rights and access to health care?" Absolutely, I told her, but I also needed something from her. Could she give us white women to speak up for a black woman's right to vote? She said she'd do it herself. We went on a national talk show together. When the host asked Janet about Planned Parenthood, she said, "I'm actually here today to talk about voting rights." When she turned to me as a representative of the NAACP and asked about voting, I said, "I'm actually here today to talk about women's rights and access to health care." This fusion coalition had brought us together, confusing old dividing lines and making more than one interviewer stutter as they tried to figure out new categories to name what was happening. "This is the LORD's doing," I told the crowd that day. "And it is marvelous in our eyes."

Without a doubt, we still had some steep hills to climb before we crossed the snake line and brought a majority of our legislators with us to the higher ground of fusion politics, but I knew by the end of 2013 that we'd passed a tipping point. Our state-based movement had necessarily focused on state government through local grassroots organizing.

From the beginning, we'd taken the long view, knowing we could not measure our success by any one election or struggle, but must measure it by our capacity to stay together and build strength. Now, through Moral Mondays, we had an opportunity to take this moral movement to the nation. Just as the Montgomery bus boycott had been about much more than public transportation in one Southern city, our struggle in North Carolina was about more than winning seats in the legislature. It was about exposing the conspiracy of the governing elite to maintain absolute power through divide-and-conquer strategies. And it was about overcoming the fears they'd played upon for decades to become what, at our best, we all hope and pray to be.

On that thirteenth Moral Monday—the last Monday in July—we announced that we would commemorate the fiftieth anniversary of the March on Washington for Jobs and Justice by holding thirteen simultaneous Take the Dream Home rallies across North Carolina. What we had done in Raleigh we would go back and do in every congressional district in the state. We would do it to make clear to our elected representatives that they could not run away from our movement by adjourning and going home. But we would also do it as a statement to the nation: we cannot fulfill Dr. King's dream by building monuments and holding commemorations in Washington, DC. No, we must heed what he said and go home. Because the battle for the soul of America is being fought at the state level, and nothing short of a moral movement converging in every state capital will make possible the reconstruction we need to fulfill our nation's promise.

CHAPTER 9

America's Third Reconstruction

MOVEMENTS TEACH YOU to make plans and then remake them on the go. This is one of the reasons why artists have always been so essential to America's freedom movements. Any artist will tell you that you can't become proficient in an art without careful attention to the masters. You have to know your history, practice the moves of those who've gone before you, and make their music your own. But you haven't mastered the art until you've learned to improvise—to take the wisdom passed down to you and write the next verse of humanity's collective song. The art of improvisation is about negotiating the unexpected.

No sooner had we laid out a plan to take the dream home to North Carolina's thirteen congressional districts than I got a call from Tim Tyson, my cellmate from the Wake County struggle. Tim said he had heard from some folks in the western part of the state who wanted us to bring Moral Mondays to the mountains. They didn't want to wait a month to host a Take the Dream Home rally. They wanted to know if I would come to Mitchell County that next Sunday evening, then lead a Moral Monday on the public square in Asheville the following day.

I remembered from my time as chair of the Human Relations Commission that Mitchell County was one of the places I'd been told to never drive at night. Back in the 1920s, after a black man was accused of rape in that part of the state, they had put all the black folks on one train and shipped them out of Mitchell County. I believe in fusion politics, but this sounded like a suicide mission. I told Tim we had a plan for the next month and we needed to stick with it.

Not long after I'd hung up the phone, Tim's daddy, the Reverend Vernon Tyson, called me. The Reverend Tyson is about eighty years old and a stalwart supporter of the movement. He started talking in a way that only an old Southern gentleman can. "Reverend Barber, I heard you don't want to go to Mitchell County, and I understand. But I've been preaching this gospel a long time, brother. I preached it in Methodist churches that I knew were run by the Klan. I know how hard it can be, Reverend Barber, so I called to let you know I'm coming with you to Mitchell County." Since he was coming with me, I knew I'd have to go. With two generations of Tysons, a couple of other folks from the movement, and our new NAACP field secretary, Laurel Ashton, we set out to test fusion politics in a county that's 99 percent white and 89 percent Republican.

When we got to the church it was packed full of white folk. The Reverend Tyson, a well known elder minister in North Carolina, introduced me, and I got up and told the story of the Moral Mondays movement in North Carolina, from that first HKonJ up to the present. I talked for nearly an hour, and the people just sat there, listening. When I was finished, one woman stood up and said, "Reverend Barber, we want you to know that we've been coming down to Moral Mondays and watching what was going on in Raleigh. We're old Eisenhower Republicans, and we know the Tea Party doesn't represent us. But we needed to make sure this whole 'Moral Monday' business wasn't just a scheme of the Democratic Party."

She sat down and another man stood up. "I'm the former chair of the Republican Party in this county," he said, "but I came tonight to tell you that I've just resigned. Our party has been taken over by extremists. It doesn't represent me anymore."

Then another stood up and said, "Reverend Barber, though we don't have any black people, we've decided to start a branch of the NAACP here in Mitchell County."

I almost fell out of my seat. In the most unlikely of places, white people were coming together to establish a local branch of America's oldest antiracist organization. Caught up in the moment, one man in the congregation stood to his feet and said, "Reverend Barber, will you lead us down the road to the home of the man who heads the Tea Party? Let's march to his house and show him that we're not going to take it anymore."

I said, "Brother, let me tell you something black folk learned a long time ago: we don't march at night." I invited them to join us the next day in downtown Asheville, and we all held hands to sing "Blessed Be the Tie That Binds."

We'd seen with our own eyes in one little church what fusion organizing could do, but I was still worried about a Moral Monday in the mountains. For weeks our critics had said, "Sure, you can get thousands of folks to come out in the progressive Triangle, but the rest of the state is red." North Carolina's mountains are populated by independent, conservative folks. To be honest, I was worried we hadn't had enough meetings like the one the night before to mobilize the mountains for a People's Assembly. I told the media we were expecting a few hundred people.

But as I was getting ready at the hotel, a young brother traveling with me came in and said, "Doc, you better hurry up. The street's so full I'm not sure we're going to be able to get out of here." At first I thought there must have been an accident. But when we finally got out to the plaza at the center of town, I looked out and saw over ten thousand people packed together, spilling out into every side street. Our first Monday out of Raleigh, we were showing America that this moral movement could go anywhere. The white woman who introduced me said, "We have a saying up here in the mountains: Don't poke the bear. Well, the extremists have poked the bear," she said. "They've woken us up, and we're ready to fight!"

It was no accident that the following year, in a midterm election when gerrymandering had all but guaranteed that most extremists would hold on to the seats that had been bought for them in America's statehouses, two of the very few Tea Party candidates in the country to be voted out of office were in North Carolina's mountains. It hadn't been in our plan, but our trip to the mountains helped me see that something much bigger than North Carolina was happening through Moral Mondays. The language, look, and longevity of these protests were tapping into our best history to show America the way forward toward a Third Reconstruction.

As we continued to build out our Forward Together Moral Movement in North Carolina, making unlikely friends from the mountains to the coast, we also started getting calls from South Carolina and Georgia, Missouri and Wisconsin. Extremists funded by dark money were introducing the same ALEC-sponsored legislation we were fighting in North Carolina. People would say, "We want to have a Moral Monday here. Will you come and be our speaker?" The first thing we had to make clear was that fusion organizing always takes the long view. There's no such thing as *a* Moral Monday. What's more, a state-based, state-government-focused fusion coalition needs indigenous leadership. I could lead in North Carolina because I was raised in North Carolina, went to school in North Carolina, pastored and organized my whole life in North Carolina, lived and breathed North Carolina. We'd spent years helping our own people realize that we couldn't wait for leadership from somewhere else to come and save us; we were the ones we had been waiting for. It was our time now.

So I wasn't about to helicopter into someone else's context and pretend to be an expert just as our coalition building was beginning to gain ground in North Carolina. No, the movement didn't need another national spokesperson to fly in and out of every tragedy, feeding the media the buzzwords we are all used to hearing. What we needed, more than anything, was a fresh vision for how a moral fusion movement could help America realize her unfulfilled promises. I started telling folks who called that I wouldn't come speak at a press conference, but I would bring a team to teach and train others in moral fusion organizing. What we had been given in North Carolina wasn't ours to hold on to; it was a gift to be shared.

To understand a moral movement, people who were accustomed to the language of Republican and Democrat, left and right, would have to first learn freedom movement history. You couldn't understand America's deep need for a Third Reconstruction without studying our history of partial progress, which has been met, time and again, by immoral acts of deconstruction. In North Carolina, we'd looked back to the state constitutional convention, in 1868, following the Civil War, where the Reverends Ashley and Hood—one white and one black—had worked tirelessly to codify the language of fusion politics in our state's primary legal document. Such cooperation could not have been possible if Frederick Douglass and Harriet Tubman had fought alone for their freedom. They built power throughout the nineteenth century by working with allies such as Levi Coffin, the white Quaker from Greensboro, North Carolina, who helped to establish the Underground Railroad. As Fergus Bordewich has chronicled in his epic history, *Bound for Canaan,* the abolitionist movement was a morally rooted, religiously inspired fusion coalition from the beginning.[1]

This was the movement that created Robert Ashley, J. W. Hood, and dozens of other leaders in America's First Reconstruction. Building their movement took decades, but when they finally came to power, they had the necessary language to begin mending the gaps in the fabric of America's democratic experiment. "We hold it to be self-evident that all persons are created equal," they wrote in North Carolina's constitution. Yes, they were two men, but they were men who'd learned to see new possibilities while singing freedom's song. They couldn't say, as their forefathers had, only that all *men* are created equal. They looked ahead to a day when their sisters would join them as full citizens of our state and wrote "all persons." They didn't throw out the best of Jefferson's language; they retained it, because they loved their enemy well enough to learn from him. But their struggle had taught them to name what a slave-holding Southern gentleman could not—that all persons are "endowed by their Creator with certain inalienable rights; among which are life, liberty, *the enjoyment of the fruit of their own labor*, and the pursuit of happiness" (emphasis mine). Workers' rights became part of North Carolina's constitution when former slaves were at the table during America's First Reconstruction.

Between 1865 and 1900, interracial alliances in every Southern state arose to advance public education, protect the right to vote, and curb corporate power by reaching across the color line. These fusion coalitions outraged white Democrats because they led to raising taxes for public education. The fusion coalitions attacked the divisive rhetoric of white solidarity and pointed out the common interests of most black and white Southerners. As the fusion coalitions gained traction, more than a quarter of white voters in the South cast their ballots for interracial coalitions and the coalitions started to take political power. In the 1890s, a fusion coalition of Republicans and Populists in North Carolina swept the state legislature, won both US Senate seats, and took the governorship. Together with their counterparts in other Southern states, these blacks and whites working together in the South passed some of the most progressive educational and labor laws in our nation's history.[2]

But fusion politics in the South was met with a violent backlash. As these coalitions began to emerge, extremists who called themselves Redeemers started a campaign to "redeem" America from the influence of black political power and progress. Exploiting religious language, this "Redemption" movement's aim was to "redeem" the South from Reconstruction, and it launched a frontal attack of immoral deconstruction. They immediately sought to deny the vote to blacks through violence, intimidation, and the passage of laws that, together, came to be called Jim Crow—a systematic, de jure denial of equality and rights, often achieved via the concept of "separate but equal." From 1890 to 1908, ten Southern states wrote new constitutions with provisions that included literacy tests, poll taxes, and grandfather clauses that denied black people the franchise not because they were black but because their enslaved grandfathers had not been able to vote. Starting in 1875, these state provisions were upheld by an ultraconservative, radical Supreme Court. Later, in the twentieth century, when the Supreme Court began to find a few of the provisions unconstitutional, states reacted rapidly in devising new legislation to continue the disenfranchisement of most blacks.[3]

Everywhere and always, the Redeemers howled about the use of tax money to support public education, especially for black children, and sought to suppress the African American vote. Driven by fear, they incited "race riots" in New Orleans, Wilmington, Atlanta, Springfield, and other cities, arming poor whites and playing on old fears in order to destroy interracial democracy and create a Jim Crow political economy rooted in low taxes, low wages, and fewer and fewer voters.[4]

When we pay attention to this history, a pattern emerges: first, the Redeemers attacked voting rights. Then they attacked public education, labor, fair tax policies, and progressive leaders. Then they took over the state and federal courts, so they could be used to render rulings that would undermine the hope of a new America. This effort culminated in the landmark case *Plessy v. Ferguson* in 1896, which upheld the constitutionality of state laws requiring segregation of public facilities under the doctrine "separate but equal." And then they made sure that certain elements had guns so that they could return the South back to the status quo ante, according to their deconstructive immoral philosophy.

Past is prologue: This history lays out how efforts to stop fusion movements have always consisted of direct acts of deconstruction on these fronts. We can see the same pattern recurring if we examine America's Second Reconstruction—what we commonly refer to as the civil rights movement. Once again, Dr. King and Rosa Parks did not launch our Second Reconstruction alone. From the very beginning of Jim Crow, there were pockets of resistance and efforts to build fusion coalitions against Jim Crow's injustice. Black and white stood together within the NAACP to protest lynching and develop legal challenges to segregated education. Small pockets of labor in the South continued to organize

across the color line. Faith-rooted radicals such as Clarence Jordan de-
fied Jim Crow; Jordan started an interracial community in Georgia in
1942. Like the abolitionists before them, these freedom fighters built
coalitions and established interracial institutions, such as Highlander
Folk School, that invested in building strength for the long haul.

As a mass movement, we can pin the beginning of the Second
Reconstruction to two specific events: the Supreme Court's *Brown v.
Board of Education* decision in 1954, and the murder of Emmett Till in
1955. *Brown* had a profound and indelible impact on the United States.
Declared the "case of the century," it established that intentional segregation was unconstitutional. This ruling served to fuel the struggle for
civil rights and equal protection under the law, challenging the legiti-
macy of all public institutions that embraced segregation. But given the
Court's lack of firm resolve, as evidenced in its refusal to order an im-
mediate injunction against segregation, public resistance to following its
mandate was inevitable.[5] The lynching of Emmett Till, a fourteen-year-
old boy from Chicago who was visiting family in Money, Mississippi, was
a vicious sign of that resistance. Till's mother refused to mourn quietly,
insisting on a public, open-casket funeral for her mutilated child. Pho-
tos from Till's funeral were published in national magazines, exposing
the violence of the Jim Crow South. Rosa Parks, a seasoned freedom
fighter who had attended trainings at Highlander, was devastated by
Till's lynching. She said she kept her seat on a Montgomery bus in part
to protest his murder.[6]

As the logo of the Student Nonviolent Coordinating Committee
captured so well with its image of white and black hands clasped together, the Second Reconstruction's power was in cross-racial, cross-
class solidarity, embracing Chicano workers, Jewish students, Native
American sister and brothers, Malcolm X's challenge, and the Poor
People's Campaign. What happened when they all got together? President John F. Kennedy issued Executive Order 10925, mandating that
projects financed with federal funds "take affirmative action" to ensure
that hiring and employment practices be free of racial bias, and we saw

the establishment of an Equal Employment Opportunity Commission. We saw civil rights connected to economic justice in the Social Security amendments of 1965, which allowed the domestic community and the agrarian communities to receive benefits that had been available for a generation to other workers. We saw the Civil Rights Act of 1964 and the Voting Rights Act of 1965. President Johnson said on August 6, 1965, that the Voting Rights Act was a triumph for freedom as huge as any victory that's ever been won on any battlefield.

But LBJ didn't say "We shall overcome" in a sudden moment of inspiration. It was a moral fusion movement that had moved him. His support for the Voting Rights Act was in direct response to the coordinated organizing of Dr. King's Southern Christian Leadership Conference, SNCC, and local leaders in Selma, Alabama. The Selma campaign grabbed the nation's attention as they watched unarmed, nonviolent marchers gassed, chased, and beaten with billy clubs on the Edmund Pettus Bridge. When people of all different faiths and colors came together and demanded change from a moral perspective, it touched the conscience of the nation. Moral fusion politics gained tremendous ground in the Second Reconstruction.

But once again, as in the 1800s, the transformative power of moral fusion politics came under attack. For a while, opponents tried the old terrorist tactics of deconstruction. They killed the four little girls in a church bombing in Birmingham, JFK in Dallas, Medgar Evers, Jimmy Lee Jackson, Viola Liuzzo, Jonathan Daniels, Malcolm X, Martin Luther King, RFK, Goodman, Schwerner, and Chaney, and others, on top of the thousands they beat, bombed, threatened, and jailed. But the great power of the Second Reconstruction was that it could not be deterred by violence. Nonviolence turned violent attacks on their head, using them to gain the moral high ground. So the extremists retooled. This is when Jim Crow went to law school and got respectable. Kevin Phillips and others began to develop the Southern Strategy, marrying old fears deeply held in the South to the self-interest of the Sun Belt and the suburbs. This is when Charles Koch stopped trying to attack the civil rights movement head-on and started investing in infrastructure. Lee Atwater, who mastered deconstruction's new tactics and became a chief Republican strategist, said in an interview years later:

> You start out in 1954 by saying, "Nigger, nigger, nigger." By 1968, you can't say "nigger"—that hurts you. Backfires. So you say stuff like forced busing. States' rights and all that stuff. You're getting so abstract now [that] you're talking about cutting taxes, and all these things you're talking about are totally economic things and a by-product of them is [that] blacks get hurt worse than whites.[7]

By using such abstractions, extremists were able to commit attention violence, holding on to power by manipulating old fears to divide and conquer people whenever we started to come together on one issue or another. But if you get down in the weeds and read the policies they implemented, the characteristic patterns of the old deconstruction are there: they used the new tools to attack voting rights, public education, fair tax structures, labor rights, women, immigrants, and minorities. Once again, they distorted religious language, declaring a New Beginning when America would once again shine as a "city on a hill." They even called themselves a "Moral Majority," as Ronald Reagan, their candidate for president, launched his campaign in Neshoba County, Mississippi, talking about "states' rights" on the hallowed ground where the civil rights workers Andrew Goodman, Michael Schwerner, and James Earl Chaney had spilled their blood in 1964 to challenge a state that would not acknowledge black people's humanity.

Though some of my friends said I sounded like a professor, I knew that folks who saw a need for change in America had to know this history. The more we paid attention to the patterns of the First and Second Reconstructions, the more our experience in North Carolina made sense. Back in 2008, our little fusion coalition, hardly a year old, had shaken the nation's governing elite to the core. With the hidden violence of their new version of the Southern Strategy, they thought they had won the battle against reconstruction once and for all. Maybe they would give a nod to democracy now and then, talking about reform on one issue or another. But they had buried the Second Reconstruction in an unmarked grave. This was *their* nation, after all.

But then a black man moved into the White House, a residence built by slaves. Fears that had been cynically manipulated for so long began to spill out not only on blogs and bar stools, but also on the floor of Congress. Though our coalition building in North Carolina had been as local and grassroots as the militiamen who were defending their homes at Lexington and Concord in 1775, the election of 2008 resounded as a shot heard round the world. When President Obama won North Carolina, that new electorate revealed the potential of a new fusion majority in this country. We'd been catching hell in North Carolina ever since because we had literally scared the hell out of them.

In both the First and the Second Reconstructions, it took the extremists more than a decade to mount an effective reaction. But in the face of this new electorate in the South, the extremists reacted immediately. In North Carolina we witnessed firsthand the development of an extreme effort that America's governing elites are now trying to effect in every state of the Union. But from the start we also recognized this opposition as a confirmation of something much more important: we are participating in the embryonic stages of a Third Reconstruction.

As I've traveled to share North Carolina's story, I've seen how a reconstruction framework can help America see our struggles in a new light. Everywhere we've gone—from deep in the heart of Dixie to Wisconsin, where I saw water frozen in waves for the first time—I heard a longing for a moral movement that plows deep into our souls and recognizes that the attacks we face today are not a sign of our weakness, but rather the manifestation of a worrisome fear among the governing elites that their days are numbered and the hour is late.

Sharing the story of North Carolina's Forward Together Moral Movement, we've had the opportunity to drink from tributaries that run toward the great stream of justice throughout America—whether in the Hands Up, Don't Shoot, I Can't Breathe, and Black Lives Matter movements; the fast-food workers' Raise Up and minimum wage movements; the voting rights and People Over Money movements; the women's rights and End Rape Culture movements; the LGBTQ equality movements; the global movement to address climate change; or the immigrant rights, Not One More movements. Within the framework of a Third Reconstruction, we see how all of our movements are flowing together, recognizing that our intersectionality creates the opportunity to fundamentally redirect America.

Within two years of our first Moral Monday in Raleigh, we saw Moral Mondays movement coalitions come together in fourteen states, not only in the South but also in the Midwest, New York, and Maine. Even as our North Carolina coalition partners organized over two hundred events, rallies, and protests across the state, the Moral Mondays movement was taken up and extended in other states, growing beyond our ability to keep count. Ours is a movement raising up leaders, not an organization recruiting followers.

If we refuse to be divided by fear and continue pushing forward together, I have no doubt that these nascent movements will swell into a Third Reconstruction to push America toward our truest hope of a "more perfect union" where peace is established through justice, not fear. This is not blind faith. We have seen it in North Carolina. We have seen it throughout America's history. And we are witnessing it even now in state-based, state-government-focused moral fusion coalitions that are gathering to stand against immoral deconstruction. Ours is the living hope of America's black-led freedom struggle, summed up so well in Langston Hughes's memorable claim that although America had never been America to him, even still he could swear, "America will be!"

Despite the dark money, old fears, and vicious attacks of extremists, we know America will be because our deepest moral values are rooted in something greater than people's ability to conspire. All the money in the world can't change that bedrock truth. This is the confidence that has sustained every moral movement in the history of the world.

In 1857, when the Supreme Court ruled in its *Dred Scott* decision that a black man had no standing in America's courts, Frederick Douglass said:

> In one point of view, we, the abolitionists and colored people, should meet this decision, unlooked for and monstrous as it appears, in a cheerful spirit. This very attempt to blot out forever the hopes of an enslaved people may be one necessary link in the chain of events preparatory to the downfall and complete overthrow of the whole slave system.
>
> The whole history of the anti-slavery movement is studded with proof that all measures devised and executed with a view to ally and diminish the anti-slavery agitation, have only served to increase, intensify, and embolden that agitation.[8]

He was right, of course. But he was speaking a long eight years before the end of the Civil War. Only as we reconstruct this moral movement mentality can we begin to shift the conscience of the nation. But we know as surely as Douglass did in 1857 that we will. We've not won yet, but we are gaining ground. When we started Moral Mondays in North Carolina, most of the issues we supported didn't have majority support in the polls. But after we shifted the public consciousness by engaging in moral critique, 55 percent of North Carolinians oppose refusing federal aid for the long-term jobless and the unemployed.[9] Fifty-five percent of North Carolinians support raising the minimum wage. Fifty-eight percent of North Carolinians say we should accept federal funds to expand Medicaid. Sixty-one percent of North Carolinians oppose using public funds for vouchers to support private schools. Fifty-four percent of North Carolinians now would rather raise taxes and give teachers a pay raise than cut taxes. Sixty-six percent of North Carolinians now don't agree with the North Carolina legislators' strict limits on women's reproductive rights. Only 33 percent agree with cutting funding for pre-kindergarten education and child care. Fewer than 25 percent agree with repealing the Racial Justice Act. Seventy-three percent favor outlawing discrimination against gays in hiring and firing, and 68 percent of voters oppose cutting early voting and favor an alternative to voter ID.

After the 2014 elections, when the extremists held on to power and succeeded in sending their leader, Thom Tillis, to the US Senate, some suggested we had failed by not running Forward Together Moral Movement candidates who would champion our agenda. But a reconstruction framework helps us to see that we will not win by starting a third party. We will win by changing the conversation for every candidate and party. To be sure, we're not there yet. But if we reconstruct a movement mentality that begins to create a public consensus about what is acceptable, then we will see a reconstruction of the legal and statutory protections that establish justice and ensure the common good.

Indeed, this is already beginning to happen. At home in North Carolina, we've seen local people's assemblies emerge in "conservative" districts, changing the conversation in places that are bright red on any political strategist's map. When we educate people about how our state's refusal to expand Medicaid is closing rural hospitals and killing white people just the same as black people, they don't follow the party line. They see how their own health is tied to the well-being of others.

As we've walked with service workers, framing their life-and-death struggle as a moral issue, we see living-wage campaigns becoming a ballot issue. When public opinion gets ahead of the party line, we need to put the question directly to the people.

Likewise with education. We've seen that we have to expose the connections between "community schools" or voucher programs and resegregation. Fully funded public education is a bedrock of multicultural democracy. In North Carolina, our constitution has provided legal grounds for this argument. But it is an essential moral issue in every state.

As our coalitions move from a new moral consensus toward legal and statutory changes, we know we have to put faces on the issues that our partners care about. We cannot be abstract. Directly affected people must lead the way and we must support and stand with them. While we continue to petition for Medicaid expansion in North Carolina and in a score of other states, we are convening People's Grand Juries to hear testimonies of citizens who are suffering because their elected officials are failing to uphold their oaths of office.

Even as we focus on real people's lives and stories, we must work to help people see how their issues are connected. Constitutional marriage amendments and so-called "religious freedom bills" must be exposed as a cynical political ploy to exploit religious convictions to divide gay folks from black folks. When any of us suffer, all of us suffer. We must stand together.

The same is true in our criminal justice system. The Third Reconstruction must abolish the death penalty in America on grounds of its unjust application. But this cannot be narrowly defined as an abolitionist struggle in which convicted killers are pitted against victim's family members. We must end the death penalty instead as a first step toward dismantling America's system of mass incarceration, which has rightly been called a "new Jim Crow." We cannot do this without reexamining three-strikes-you're-out laws and a broken plea-bargaining system in which prosecutors elected by a white-majority electorate in counties have unchecked power in over-policed inner-city neighborhoods.

Because political power is a democracy's chief safeguard against injustice, we must continue to engage the voting rights issue after the US Supreme Court's decision in *Shelby County v. Holder*, which removed protections against voter suppression in Southern states that had been in place for half a century. This fight is, in many ways, bigger than Selma and the Voting Rights Act of 1965. That expansion of voting rights fifty years ago was a concession to the civil rights movement. We didn't get all we were asking for. Now, fifty years later, we're fighting to hold on to the compromise. What we really need is a constitutional amendment to guarantee the same voting rights in every state. This must be a cornerstone of the Third Reconstruction.

In the church where I was raised, the old folks used to sing a song with the words, "Hold on just a little while longer . . . every little thing is gonna be all right." Holding on to that faith, moral movements have never known ahead of time how long we would have to struggle before we reach higher ground. But we've always known that, when we get there, every little thing is gonna be all right. So we hold on to faith and take care of one another as we travel on this way. And lest we get distracted by the snares and cares of this world, we say to one another, "Forward together! Not one step back!"

Fourteen Steps
Forward Together

AMERICA'S THIRD RECONSTRUCTION depends on a moral movement, deeply rooted in the South, emerging state by state throughout the nation. No single leader or organization can orchestrate such a movement, but we who have seen the power of fusion organizing in North Carolina in 2014 established an education center, Repairers of the Breach, to share the lessons of Moral Mondays and invest in equipping leaders for other state-based coalitions. In order to move forward together, we've outlined fourteen steps to mobilize in the streets, at the polls, and in the courtroom.

1. **Engage in indigenously led grassroots organizing across the state.** There is no end run around the relational work of building trust and empowering local people. Crises will bring out crowds and draw attention, but a sustained movement depends on local people who know one another and are committed to working together for the long haul. "Helicopter" leadership by "national leaders" will not sustain a moral movement. Equip and resource small groups of people who will meet regularly in their home communities to talk about the coalition's concerns.

2. **Use moral language to frame and critique public policy, regardless of who is in power.** A moral movement claims higher ground in partisan debate by returning public discourse to our deepest moral and constitutional values. Any moral movement must study Scripture and sacred texts as well as state constitutions. We cannot allow so-called conservatives to hijack the powerful language of faith; neither can we let so-called liberals pretend that moral convictions are not at play in public policy debates. Every budget is a moral document—or it is an immoral one. We must reclaim moral language in the public square.

3. **Demonstrate a commitment to civil disobedience that follows the steps of nonviolent action and is designed to change the public conversation and consciousness.** A moral movement draws power not from its ability to overwhelm opposition but from its willingness to suffer. The Second Reconstruction brought large-scale nonviolent direct action to America through the Montgomery bus boycott. A Third Reconstruction depends upon escalating noncooperation in order to demonstrate our capacity to sacrifice for a better future.

4. **Build a stage from which to lift the voices of everyday people impacted by immoral policies.** A moral movement must put human faces on injustice and amplify the voice of the voiceless. We do not speak for those who can speak for themselves. We do not create a platform for politicians to speak for those who can speak for themselves. Directly affected people are the best moral witnesses. Our movement exists to let their voices be heard.

5. **Recognize the centrality of race.** America's First and Second Reconstructions sought to heal the wound of race-based slavery, America's original sin. Our Third Reconstruction must likewise be decidedly antiracist. Some will ask, Is the real issue today race or is it class? We answer: Yes, it's race *and* class. Our class divisions cannot be understood apart from a society built on white supremacy.

Our moral movement must be committed to the long-term work of racial equity.

6. **Build a broad, diverse coalition including moral and religious leaders of all faiths.** All faith traditions are not the same, but the common ground among faiths is a firm foundation upon which to stand against the divide-and-conquer strategies of extremists. We must be intentional about reaching out to marginalized groups in our states. Though they are a minority in this country, our Muslim sisters and brothers are essential to the Third Reconstruction.

7. **Intentionally diversify the movement with the goal of winning unlikely allies.** Often the groups most impacted by injustice have been convinced that they are enemies. Fusion politics is about helping those who have suffered injustice and have been divided by extremism to see what we have in common. We do this by bringing people together across dividing lines and helping them hear one another. We have no permanent enemies, only permanent issues, rooted in our deepest moral and constitutional values.

8. **Build transformative, long-term coalition relationships rooted in a clear agenda that doesn't measure success only by electoral outcomes.** We must be clear: Fusion coalitions are not about simple transactions where I support your issue if you support mine. We must learn how our issues intersect in a comprehensive moral agenda that demands transformation of everyone—not least, of us.

9. **Make a serious commitment to academic and empirical analysis of policy.** Nothing is worse than being loud and wrong. Our coalitions must include activist scholars and we must commit ourselves to a serious consideration of data. Moral issues are not impractical. They can be translated into policy that is sustainable and that produces measurable positive outcomes.

10. **Coordinate use of all forms of social media: video, text, Twitter, Facebook, and so forth.** Mainstream media outlets are often unable

to tell a story that doesn't fit within the established narrative. We must tell our own story. Social media afford us multiple outlets for the consciousness-raising that movements have always depended upon. Use them all.

11. **Engage in voter registration and education.** The political power of fusion coalitions is based upon a diversified electorate that recognizes common interests. Extremists understand this. They have invested heavily in restricting voting rights and dividing potential allies. We must engage voters in each election, educating them about how candidates have voted or committed to vote on issues that are part of our shared moral agenda.

12. **Pursue a strong legal strategy.** A moral movement rooted in constitutional values needs a strong legal team and a commitment to mobilizing in the courtroom. The future we imagine and embody in the streets must be established in our statehouses and affirmed by our courts. We cannot neglect this key piece of our common life.

13. **Engage the cultural arts.** A moral movement is only as strong as the songs we sing together. Study the history of cultural arts in freedom movements and bring music, the spoken word, storytelling, and visual arts into your organizing. Make sure the images in your art and actions convey the same message you are proclaiming with words. Speak the truth, sing the truth, and use art to help people imagine the future they cannot yet see.

14. **Resist the "one moment" mentality; we are building a movement!** No one victory will usher in beloved community; no single setback can stop us. We are building up a new world, moving forward together toward freedom and justice for all.

To learn more about training for moral fusion organizing, visit www.breach repairers.org.

The purpose of voter suppression is unconstitutional you are violating the 14th Amendment.

The supreme court are attacking LGPT, public education and safety net for the poor. Dr. Moral Monday is espically important.

IN THE SUMMER OF 2013, as Moral Mondays became a national news story, I stood on the edges of this protest-turned-revival-meeting and watched the most diverse congregation of people I've witnessed in my lifetime, electrified week after week by the Reverend Barber's sermons. Rooted in the black prophetic preaching tradition, his sermons were crafted for the public square—unashamedly confessional, yet at the same time radically inclusive. Like all good Southern revival sermons, each one ended with an altar call. Only here, in the context of a moral crisis at our statehouse, the invitation to come forward was a call to nonviolent direct action. Hundreds responded, week after week, joyfully submitting to an evening in jail. The Tuesday morning I walked out of the Wake County Detention Center, I was greeted by dozens of supporters, warm hugs, and a delicious baked ziti. Someone handed me a button that said, "I WENT TO JAIL WITH REV. BARBER."

This wasn't the first time I'd been arrested by the Reverend Barber's preaching. As a Southern Baptist kid growing up in North Carolina two decades earlier, I had been a young Republican who wanted to join the Moral Majority. I went to work in the US Senate and paged for Strom Thurmond. Rooming with a congressman's son on Capitol Hill, I thought I was on my way to a career in conservative politics. But

NO
NO
NO

something wasn't quite right. I couldn't reconcile the realities of DC politics with the words of Jesus I'd memorized in church. I came home thinking there must be a better way.

A few months later, I attended an event in North Carolina hosted by the governor's office. The keynote speaker for the evening was the chair of the Human Relations Commission, William J. Barber II. I didn't know he was a preacher when he stepped to the podium. But by the time he sat down, a ballroom full of people were on their feet, clapping and shouting like a Pentecostal camp meeting. I was among them. Unsure what had happened to us, I knew I had to hear more from this man.

When I invited the Reverend Barber to come preach at my home church in Stokes County, he graciously accepted. But he did not come alone. He told me he wouldn't come to my hometown by himself because he knew its history. I was from Klan country and didn't even know it.

As a native son of North Carolina, I count it one of the great gifts of my life that I was befriended and, in the very best sense of the word, *pastored* by the Reverend Barber. For him, fusion politics is no mere political theater. It has been the substance of his faith for the twenty years I've known him. It's what drew me to him that night in a hotel ballroom and it's what most impresses me about his life and vision still.

As media outlets from the *New York Times* to Fox News sent reporters to cover the Moral Mondays story, the Reverend Barber and I talked about problems with how this story was being told. The trouble wasn't the individual reporters themselves. Many of them were good journalists who worked hard to tell the story they could see. But the limited left-right framework of the twenty-four-hour news cycle made it difficult for them to name what was happening, where it had come from, and what it might offer beyond North Carolina. Whether they considered themselves Republican, Democrat, or independent, the people who showed up at Moral Mondays got it. They went home and told their friends, and the movement continued to grow more diverse. It became clear that a new justice movement was rising up from the soil of grassroots organizing here in North Carolina. If a Third Reconstruction could take root here, we knew it could happen anywhere.

But the greatest danger to a Third Reconstruction was that people might not recognize it. Because they did not know the long history of coalition building here in North Carolina, many reporters saw Moral Mondays as a spontaneous response to particular legislation. When that act of protest did not immediately effect the change they thought it aimed to bring about, it was easy to dismiss. Reporters pointed ahead to the midterm elections of 2014, saying over and again that they would be a referendum on North Carolina's legislature. But we had put our bodies on the line to say that the redistricting and voter suppression in Raleigh were an attack on the democratic process itself. In 2008, the largest turnout in North Carolina's history of poor and African American voters had prompted this extremist backlash. Whether we were winning or losing depended on how you told the story. In the context of the long struggle for justice in this country, we knew this was a story of hope.

On his fiftieth birthday, at the end of the long summer of 2013, I sat down with the Reverend Barber and recorded the interviews that provided the basic outline of this book. In the course of that day, we were interrupted only once, by a reporter who tracked him down at my office. It would prove to be a rare respite. As I worked to write this story, we scheduled follow-up interviews in which I checked facts, probed the Reverend Barber's memory, and sought clarity about his vision. We often met when he was on his way to or from the airport, sharing the movement with others even as he studied what was happening in their places. Our conversations mixed with calls from people on the ground in Ferguson, aides at the White House, lawyers reporting on challenges in the courts, reporters asking for a quote. And those were just the people who had his cell phone number. A few times we tried to continue a conversation while walking down the street in Durham. Without explanation, people would stop us to ask if they could have their picture taken with the Reverend Barber. A homeless man stopped us to give a detailed report of police brutality. To each of them Reverend Barber extended the same honest but generous hand he'd extended to me twenty years earlier. I took notes on everything. His life, I decided, was his message.

When I attended seminary, I recall learning about the authorship of biblical books. Although some of the New Testament letters were written in Paul's name, historians have pointed out that many of the issues they address did not arise until Paul himself had been dead for decades. The same with the prophet Isaiah. The most reliable scholarship suggests he was alive only during the period when the first third of the book that bears his name was recorded. Second and third Isaiah were most likely written in his voice by those who took up his mantle and carried on the work Isaiah had started.

The Reverend Barber keeps saying this is how we've written this book, and I suppose he's right. Except that he's very much alive and carrying the message forward. I'm honored to be a conduit for his words.

The process of telling this story has taught me something about fusion politics that may help other readers understand where they fit in America's Third Reconstruction. We can neither hear nor tell stories without asking ourselves along the way where we find ourselves in the story. As I've reflected on America's history since the First Reconstruction, I've had to confess that I know the fear which has created a backlash against the black-led freedom movement time and again. It was suggested in a thousand conversations I overheard growing up—and clearly stated in more than one. I cannot pretend that the resistance to what I've written here is somewhere else. I carry it within me.

But that is not all that is in me. Jesus said love can drive out fear, and I have found great hope in the way white folks have joined the black-led freedom struggle, from the abolition movement up to the present. Writing this story, I've been drawn to the voices of Angelina Grimke and Levi Coffin, Anne Braden and William Stringfellow. I've become more and more interested in the white people who said little, but were present—people like Stanley Levison, from whom Martin Luther King Jr. refused to dissociate himself, even when asked to do so by the president himself (the FBI director, J. Edgar Hoover, had convinced

President Kennedy that Levison was a Communist, manipulating King and the civil rights movement). These stories are little known, but they help people like me to see that we have a role to play in fusion politics and the Third Reconstruction.

Our job is not to take the lead, but to pledge our allegiance to the other America—the country that has not yet been but that one day shall be.

Fear is at the root of the violent backlash that the Third Reconstruction faces. I have read through the death threats the Reverend Barber receives, and I have watched the fears of white men I grew up with raging out of control. But fear is not only violent. Fear is also paralyzing, convincing so many of us that there is little we can do to change a world we know to be horribly broken. Fear whispers, "Well, that's just the way it is." Or, "These things are beyond me. I'll just do what I can to love the people where I am."

Maybe what we fear the most is that the Reverend Barber is right: that the heavy lifting to establish a multiethnic democracy isn't behind us in our Civil War or civil rights movement, but rather is very present in the Moral Movement of today. Maybe America isn't possible without a Third Reconstruction. Maybe we were born for such a time as this.

I'm willing to believe that America is possible—that fusion politics is not a pipe dream—because of a black preacher who was willing to embrace me, even when he knew I was from Klan country. That embrace was one step in a twenty-year journey. But fusion politics, as it turns out, is about one step after another into a relationship with the people who are supposed to be our enemies.

I can trust a man who embraces his enemy, then trusts him to tell his story.

Jonathan Wilson-Hartgrove

ACKNOWLEDGMENTS

LIKE ANYONE ENGAGED IN MOVEMENT WORK, I write every day—
e-mails, speeches, articles, press releases. The words I write are not
"mine"; they are an expression of the collective wisdom I've received
from countless elders, young people, sisters, and brothers in the struggle for justice. I never write or speak without knowing I have others
to thank.

But this book, in particular, has been an exercise in remembering
how central family is to my life and work in the movement. I am who I
am because of my grandmamma, my late father, for whom I was named,
and my mother, Momma Barber, who is still standing and fighting with
us today. They serve for me as concrete reminders of the ancestors
who've gone before us in the struggle, feeding a river of resistance that
makes our life and work possible.

My life is, in so many ways, sustained by the faith and love of my
wife, Rebecca, and our children, almost all of whom are now adults.
It gives me great joy to work alongside my sons and daughters today,
watching them take up for themselves the freedom movement that was
passed down to me.

2021

In addition to my biological family, I have always been part of a
church family—that worldwide community of sisters and brothers who

pray daily to "Our Father," always present to us in the particular people of local congregations. Greenleaf Christian Church has been that home church to me and my family for nearly a quarter century now. They've shown me the best of what church can be, and they have supported my ministry beyond the church walls. It is my great joy to call them family. In particular, I want to thank the team of faithful folk who are with me every day—driving me to engagements, coordinating logistics, praying with me, and loving me through the ups and downs of daily life.

Through the moral movement, I've met sisters and brothers I didn't know I had—a family that crosses every racial, political, religious, and partisan line. Some of those precious family members are named in these pages; many of them are not. But I want to thank each of them. It is a privilege to get to tell our story.

For this telling of the story, I thank Jonathan, my brother in the church and the movement, who helped me step back from the daily task of speaking to a movement in order to find words that express our work's deeper roots and broader context.

Though my brother Al McSurely's name does not appear on many pages of this book, I recall his presence—and that of his beloved wife, Ashley, gone too soon—in almost every story. Movements depend upon quiet actors like Al every bit as much as they need storytellers like me. It gives me great joy to dedicate this book to brother Al, sister Ashley, and our extended family in the Forward Together Moral Movement.

NOTES

CHAPTER 1: *Son of a Preacher Man*

1. Jürgen Moltmann, *Theology of Hope* (Minneapolis: Fortress Press, 1993), 21.
2. William J. Barber, "The Disciple Assemblies of Eastern North Carolina," master's thesis, Butler University, 1959.
3. For a brief history of the Fusion Party in North Carolina and the Wilmington, North Carolina, coup d'état of 1898, see Timothy B. Tyson, "The Ghosts of 1898: Wilmington's Race Riot and the Rise of White Supremacy," special insert, *News & Observer* (Raleigh, NC), November 17, 2006, http://media2 .newsobserver.com/content/media/2010/5/3/ghostsof1898.pdf.
4. Cornel West, *Prophesy Deliverance! An Afro-American Revolutionary Christianity* (Philadelphia: Westminster John Knox Press, 1983): "The assimilationist response to the challenges of self-image and self-determination is this: a rejection of Afro-American culture and total assimilation into American society" (78–80).
5. Proverbs 11:14 (Revised Standard Version; all Bible citations are from this version unless otherwise indicated).
6. Micah 6:8.

CHAPTER 2: *My First Fight*

1. Psalm 94:5–7.
2. Reinhold Niebuhr, *Moral Man and Immoral Society: A Study in Ethics and Politics* (Philadelphia: Westminster John Knox Press, 2002).

3. Psalm 94:16.

4. Oliver Johnson, *William Lloyd Garrison and His Times* (Boston: Houghton, Mifflin, and Company, 1881), 199–200.

5. Psalm 94:17.

6. Hebrews 10:39 (New International Version).

CHAPTER 3: *Learning to Stand Together*

1. II Corinthians 12:9.

2. Luke 4:18.

3. William Turner, "Black Evangelicalism: Theology, Politics, Race," *Journal of Religious Thought* (Howard Divinity School) 45, no. 2 (1989): 40–56.

CHAPTER 4: *From Banquets to Battle*

1. Isaiah 58:6–8.

2. Kids Count, http://datacenter.kidscount.org/.

3. Ezekiel 48:35.

4. North Carolina Constitution, Article I, Section 1, and Article XI, Section 4, http://www.ncga.state.nc.us/legislation/constitution/ncconstitution.html.

CHAPTER 5: *Resistance Is Your Confirmation*

1. Hood quoted in Sidney Andrews, *The South Since the War: 14 Weeks of Travel and Observation* (Boston: Ticknor & Fields, 1866), 122.

2. Thornburg v. Gingles, 478 U.S. 30 (1986), Justia.com, https://supreme.justia.com/cases/federal/us/478/30/case.html.

3. Citizens United v. Federal Election Commission, 558 U.S. 08–205 (2010), Justia.com, https://supreme.justia.com/cases/federal/us/558/08–205.

4. "NC House Speaker Tillis—Divide and Conquer!," YouTube, http://www.youtube.com/watch?v=O8ewESI51s4&list=PLCD69FC75ACE0EFF4; accessed May 24, 2015.

5. Luke 4:18, 29–30.

CHAPTER 6: *Many a Conflict, Many a Doubt*

1. Martin Luther King Jr., "Palm Sunday Sermon on M. K. Gandhi Delivered at Dexter Ave. Baptist Church," March 22, 1959, Martin Luther King, Jr. Research and Education Institute, https://kinginstitute.stanford.edu/king-papers/documents/palm-sunday-sermon-mohandas-k-gandhi-delivered-dexter-avenue-baptist-church.

2. Martin Luther King Jr., "The Value of Unions," speech, October 7, 1965,

Martin Luther King Center for Nonviolent Social Change, quoted in AFL-CIO report, http://www.aflcio.org/content/download/2511/24271 /King's+Speeces+to+Labor.pdf.

3. See Douglas A. Blackmon, *Slavery by Another Name* (New York: Doubleday/ Anchor, 2009). In 2012 PBS released a documentary by the same name that narrates Blackmon's groundbreaking history.

4. This argument is detailed in Michelle Alexander's *The New Jim Crow* (New York: New Press, 2010).

5. Philip J. Cook, "Potential Savings from Abolition of the Death Penalty in North Carolina," *American Law and Economics Review* 11, no. 2 (December 2009): 428–529, http://www.deathpenaltyinfo.org/documents/CookCostRpt .pdf.

6. Dr. King's most famous summary of this four-step process is in his "Letter from Birmingham Jail," TeachingAmericanHistory.org, http://teaching americanhistory.org/library/document/letter-from-birmingham-city-jail -excerpts/.

7. North Carolina Constitution, Article 1, Section 15, http://www.ncga.state .nc.us/legislation/constitution/ncconstitution.html.

8. Isaiah 10:1.

CHAPTER 7: *The Darkness Before the Dawn*

1. Jeremiah 17:9.

2. North Carolina Constitution, Article 1, Section 12.

3. Much of this was disclosed as the result of a subpoena in a suit the NAACP filed against the state. For a good summary by investigative journalists, see Olga Pierce, Justin Elliott, and Theodoric Meyer, "How Dark Money Helped Republicans Hold the House and Hurt Voters," *ProPublica*, December 21, 2012, http://www.propublica.org/article/how-dark-money-helped-republicans -hold-the-house-and-hurt-voters.

4. Luke 12:2–3.

5. Gar Alperovitz, *America Beyond Capitalism: Reclaiming Our Wealth, Our Liberty, and Our Democracy* (San Francisco: Wiley, 2006), 17.

6. These statistics and those below are from the University of North Carolina Center on Poverty, Work, and Opportunity, http://www.law.unc.edu/centers /poverty/.

7. Psalm 118:22.

8. Luke 12:11–12.

9. 2 Kings 3:15, King James Version.

CHAPTER 8: *A Moral Movement for the Nation*

1. See Taylor Branch, *Pillar of Fire: America in the King Years, 1963–1965* (New York: Simon & Schuster, 1999), 41–49.
2. Nick Wing, "Moral Monday Draws 'Moron Monday' Insult from Republican as Dozens Arrested in North Carolina," *Huffington Post*, http://www .huffingtonpost.com/2013/06/11/moral-monday-north-carolina_n_3420957 .html.
3. Psalm 118:23–24.

CHAPTER 9: *America's Third Reconstruction*

1. Fergus M. Bordewich, *Bound for Canaan: The Epic Story of the Underground Railroad, America's First Civil Rights Movement* (New York: HarperCollins/ Amistad Press, 2005).
2. Eric Foner, *A Short History of Reconstruction, 1863–1877* (New York: Harper & Row, 1990), 254–55. For the interracial Readjusters movement, see Jane Dailey, *Before Jim Crow: The Politics of Race in Postemancipation Virginia* (Chapel Hill: University of North Carolina Press, 2000), especially 1–14. See also J. Morgan Kousser, *The Shaping of Southern Politics: Suffrage Restriction and the Establishment of the One-Party South, 1880–1910* (New Haven, CT: Yale University Press, 1974), 171–75. For the fusion movement in North Carolina, see Helen G. Edmonds, *The Negro and Fusion Politics in North Carolina, 1894–1901* (Chapel Hill: University of North Carolina Press, 1951).
3. Eric Foner and John A. Garraty, eds., *The Reader's Companion to American History* (New York: Houghton Mifflin, 1991), 917–23.
4. For North Carolina, see David S. Cecelski and Timothy B. Tyson, *Democracy Betrayed: The Wilmington Race Riot and Its Legacy* (Chapel Hill: University of North Carolina Press, 1998), and H. Leon Prather, *"We Have Taken a City": The Wilmington Racial Massacre and Coup of 1898* (Cranbury, NJ: Associated University Presses, 1984). For Atlanta, see David Fort Godshalk, *Veiled Visions: The 1906 Atlanta Race Riot and the Remaking of American Race Relations* (Chapel Hill: University of North Carolina Press, 2005), and Gregory Mixon, *The Atlanta Riot: Race, Class and Violence in a New South City* (Gainesville: University of Florida Press, 2005). For Springfield, see Roberta Senechal, *The Sociogenesis of a Race Riot: Springfield, Illinois, in 1908* (Urbana: University of Illinois Press, 1990).
5. See Charles J. Ogletree Jr., *All Deliberate Speed: Reflections on the First Half Century of* Brown v. Board of Education (New York: W. W. Norton, 2004).

6. See Jeanne Theoharis, *The Rebellious Life of Mrs. Rosa Parks* (Boston: Beacon Press, 2013), chapter 3; 93.

7. Lee Atwater, quoted in Alexander P. Lamis, ed., *Southern Politics in the 1990s* (Baton Rouge: Louisiana State University Press, 1999), 8.

8. Frederick Douglass, "Speech on the Dred Scott Decision," May 1857, TeachingAmericanHistory.org, http://teachingamericanhistory.org/library /document/speech-on-the-dred-scott-decision-2.

9. Statistics in this paragraph from Public Policy Polling of North Carolina for 2013, http://www.publicpolicypolling.com/.

INDEX

Voc [handwritten: wanting or devouring great quantities of food / VORACIOUS / indigenously P.127]

[handwritten margin notes: (1) insatiable; (2) unquenchable; unappeasable; prodigious; uncontrollable; compulsive; gut; gluttonous; greedy; rapacious; avid; desirous; esurient; redundant; multiethnic P.135]

Overtly racist
p.63 As we just witness in
Rosanna O'Donald

simplisafce
Treating complex issue and problems as simpler than they really are.

interpret: translate orally the words of a person speaking a different language.

Blaxploitation: the exploitation of black people when it comes to roles in movie.

VORACIOUS

embedded

spasmodic grip

reiterated

enormity

Rejoice in the Lord always: [and] again I say, Rejoice

Phil 4:4

Always be full of joy in the Lord. Always I say it again—rejoice!